AMERICA'S *Other* AUDUBON

America's *Other* Audubon

JOY M. KISER

PRINCETON ARCHITECTURAL PRESS

NEW YORK

Published by
Princeton Architectural Press
37 East Seventh Street
New York, New York 10003

Visit our website at www.papress.com

All color plates courtesy of the Smithsonian Institution Libraries,
Washington, DC
Page 7: Nelson and his buggy,
courtesy of Steven Nelson Jonnes
Page 8: Courtesy of Steven Nelson Jonnes
Page 12: Cleveland Museum of Natural History
Page 21: Courtesy of Steven Nelson Jonnes
Page 192: Virginia's personal copy of her daughter's book, now
in the possession of the Cleveland Museum of Natural History.
It was donated to the museum by Dr. N. L. Siplock but without
the bronze medal it had been awarded in the World's Columbian
Exposition of 1893. Photograph by Bruce Frumker.

Plate XXXV, page 92
    John Maynard Wheaton, "Report on the Birds of Ohio," vol. 1, part
    1, *Report of the Geological Survey of Ohio* (Columbus, OH, 1882).
Plate XLII, page 106
    Spencer Fullerton Baird, T. M. (Thomas Mayo) Brewer, Robert
    Ridgway, *A History of North American Birds*, vol. 1, *Land Birds*
    (Boston: Little, Brown, 1905). First published in 1874.
Plate XLVII, figure 4, page 116
    Frank W. Langdon, *Journal of the Cincinnati Society of Natural
    History*, vol. XII, 1883.
Plate XLVIII, figure 1, page 118
    Elliott Coues, *Birds of the Colorado Valley; A Repository of Scientific
    and Popular Information Concerning North American Ornithology*
    (Washington, DC: Government Printing Office, 1878), 524.

Plate LX, figure 4, page 146
    Baird, Brewer, Ridgway, *A History of North American Birds*, 1:555.
Plate LXIV, figure 5, page 156
    John James Audubon, *Ornithological Biography, or an Account of
    the Habits of the Birds of the United States of America* (Philadelphia:
    Judah Dobson, 1831), 320.
Plate LXVIII, figure 3, page 164
    Oliver Davie, *An Egg Check List of North American Birds*
    (Columbus, OH: Hann & Adair, 1884).
Plate LXVIII, figure 6, page 166
    Davie, *An Egg Check List of North American Birds*, 115.
Plate LXVIII, figure 7, page 166
    C. J. Maynard, *Birds of Eastern North America* (Newtonville,
    MA: C. J. Maynard, 1881), 99.
Plate LXVIII, figure 11, page 167
    Elliott Coues, *Birds of the North-west, a Hand-book of the
    Ornithology of the Region Drained by the Missouri River
    and Its Tributaries* (Washington, DC: Washington Government
    Printing Office, 1874).

Editor: Linda Lee
Designer: Bree Anne Apperley

Special thanks to: Sara Bader, Nick Beatty, Nicola Bednarek Brower,
Janet Behning, Fannie Bushin, Megan Carey, Carina Cha,
Russell Fernandez, Jan Haux, Diane Levinson, Jennifer Lippert,
Gina Morrow, John Myers, Katharine Myers, Margaret Rogalski,
Elana Schlenker, Dan Simon, Sara Stemen, Andrew Stepanian,
Paul Wagner, and Joseph Weston of Princeton Architectural Press
—Kevin C. Lippert, publisher

Library of Congress Cataloging-in-Publication Data
Kiser, Joy M., 1947–
America's other Audubon / Joy M. Kiser. — 1st ed.
   p. cm.
ISBN 978-1-61689-059-9 (hardcover : alk. paper)
1. Jones, Genevieve (Genevieve Estelle), 1847-1879. 2.
Ornithologists—United States—Biography. 3. Birds—North
America—Pictorial works. 4. Ornithological illustration—
North America. 5. Birds in art. I. Jones, Genevieve (Genevieve
Estelle), 1847–1879. II. Title.
QL31.J59K57 2012
598.092—dc23
[B]
                                                    2011039605

CONTENTS

9   FOREWORD *by* Leslie K. Overstreet,
Smithsonian Institution Libraries

10   PREFACE

13   INTRODUCTION

23   PLATES

169   KEY TO THE EGGS

"IN THEIR EGGS THE BIRDS CENTER THEIR WHOLE EXISTENCE.
They work unceasingly and intelligently for a place where they can lay them, and guard
them with their lives. Thus the nest, aside from its expression of ingenuity, skill,
and patience, becomes an exponent of character."

Howard Jones, Introduction to *Illustrations of the Nests and Eggs of Birds of Ohio*

I dedicate this book to the memories of Ellis and Evelyn Seiberling, who always believed in me.

*

The Jones family in 1858, from left: Howard, Nelson, Genevieve (Gennie), and Virginia

FOREWORD

You are about to discover an extraordinary work of science and art and the equally extraordinary story of how it came into being.

The creation of a talented young woman and her dedicated family in a small Ohio town far from the intellectual and artistic centers of the mid-nineteenth century, *Illustrations of the Nests and Eggs of Birds of Ohio* was a singular and remarkable achievement. It is almost impossible for us today to imagine how ambitious the project was in its own time or how daunting the physical and technological obstacles that had to be dealt with and overcome. Even more, in our modern world of the professionalization of science, it may seem astonishing that amateurs like the Joneses could produce something scientifically important and lasting. But the book was appreciated immediately as a significant contribution to the developing science of American ornithology, and it remains unequaled in its field to this day.

Joy M. Kiser will tell its story in the pages that follow, and it is hers to tell, for it is she who unearthed it in that small Ohio town, in the storerooms and archives of a county historical society, and in the attics of the Jones family's descendants, almost forgotten by the rest of the world. Fifteen years ago, at her job as the librarian at the Cleveland Museum of Natural History, Joy came across a copy of the massive, two-volume book and was struck by its fusion of artistry and scientific accuracy. Her fascination developed into a serious effort to research the book, with each new bit of information fueling her curiosity. As time went on she dug deeper and deeper, exploring the time and place of the book's production, reading through hundred-year-old volumes of ornithological journals, discovering the lithographic stones and artists' palettes and brushes used to create it, and locating the family's personal letters and documents.

Joy's dedication in pursuing this research and her determination to bring the book and the Jones family to modern audiences match the original effort of its creation. As you will see, the beautiful, meticulously hand-colored illustrations and the story of the Joneses' energy, intelligence, perseverance, and sacrifice are well worth the years of exhaustive investigation that Joy undertook. The excitement of her discoveries and the satisfaction of being able to restore a neglected treasure to its well-deserved place in the history of American natural science have been deepened by the welcome and assistance that have been extended to her by the Jones family descendants, whose generosity and support have been invaluable.

The Smithsonian Institution Libraries is fortunate to hold two copies of the *Illustrations of the Nests and Eggs of Birds of Ohio*, now affectionately known among us as simply "The nests and eggs," and it was by answering Joy's query about them in 1997 that I became acquainted with her research. For over one hundred years, ornithologists at the Smithsonian's National Museum of Natural History and in similar institutions around the country have consulted the book's meticulously detailed and scientifically accurate illustrations to identify nests and eggs in museum research collections, but few beyond this specialized group even know that the book exists. Now you will have the pleasure of seeing all of the illustrations and reading the story behind them. I hope that you will find it as fascinating as I do.

Leslie K. Overstreet
Curator of Natural-History Rare Books
SMITHSONIAN INSTITUTION LIBRARIES

PREFACE

On May 22, 1995—an idyllic spring morning—I walked into the Cleveland Museum of Natural History in Ohio, full of anticipation and eager to begin my new position as assistant librarian. Volume one of *Illustrations of the Nests and Eggs of Birds of Ohio* was exhibited in a Plexiglas display case at the foot of the stairway that led to the library on the second floor. A label, about three inches high by five inches wide, succinctly explained that the book was the accomplishment of the Jones family of Ohio: the daughter, Genevieve, had conceived of the idea and had begun drawing and painting the illustrations with the assistance of a childhood friend; the son, Howard, had collected the nests and eggs; the father, Nelson, had paid the publishing costs; and after Genevieve died, the mother, Virginia, and the rest of the family spent eight years completing the work as a memorial to Genevieve.

The book was on exhibit for several weeks. Each morning as I climbed the stairs, I would gaze at the label in the case and then into the faces of the members of the Jones family, whose photographs had been tipped onto the page adjacent to the illustration being displayed in the exhibit case. I became increasingly bewildered that eight years of work could be summed up on such a tiny label in so few words, and with such a lack of emotion. I found Genevieve's face almost haunting—her large, expressive eyes full of expectancy and hope. Was this book the only thing that was left to represent her life? What kind of person was she that she would inspire her entire family to devote so much of their own lives to completing her undertaking? Surely, her story must be one filled with passion. But the exhibit came to an end, the book was returned to a climate-controlled vault far from the main library, and my thoughts about Genevieve and her family were left to simmer on the back burner in my mind.

Then in March of 1997, a dear friend passed away unexpectedly. After his funeral, I returned to work, where I encountered a notice for a conference of the international Society for the History of Natural History that had been posted on the rare book LISTSERV Exlibris by Leslie K. Overstreet, the curator of Natural-History Rare Books at the Smithsonian Institution Libraries. The conference would take place at the University of Virginia (UVA). I discussed the event with the head librarian, David Condon, and he encouraged me to apply to the Smead Staff Enrichment Fund for financial support to attend.

A few weeks later, I was on a plane flying out of a snow-covered Cleveland, and within hours I was descending into a blossom-filled spring day in Charlottesville, Virginia. The conference was fascinating. Scholars from world-renowned libraries presented papers on natural history. The attendees toured the grounds of the university, visited Monticello, and viewed Rachel Lambert Mellon's Oak Spring Garden Library, a private collection of rare books, manuscripts, works of art relating to botany, horticulture, gardening, landscape design, natural history, and travel. The sunshine, visual and intellectual stimulation, and pleasant interaction with people who shared similar interests were uplifting. The theme of the society's next conference, to be held in 1999 at the Natural History Museum in London, was natural history illustration. I remembered Genevieve's book. A search of the UVA's library catalog revealed that they owned a copy. I wondered how many other libraries had the volume in their collections.

When I returned to work, I searched the Online Computer Library Center catalog but could only locate a few libraries that owned the book. Not surprisingly, most copies of the book were held at libraries and historical societies in Ohio. The catalog description indicated that only one hundred copies had been made. The rarity of the book piqued my interest—would a research paper chronicling the creation of the illustrations for this book be unique enough to be accepted for inclusion in the London conference? It seemed likely that any primary sources that existed would be within driving distance, so the cost of doing the research would be reasonable, and I felt sure that if my paper was accepted it would bring positive attention to the library's rare-book collection.

On April 14, 1999, I gave my first professional presentation at the conference on natural history illustration in the Natural History Museum in London. It was not immediately apparent how the topic had been received. Only two women from the audience came up to say how much they had enjoyed the Jones's story. For the rest of the evening and the following morning, I wondered whether a book created by a family from a small town in Ohio was equal to the works of Alexander Wilson, Mark Catesby, or John James Audubon.

When the meeting reconvened, the conference leader opened by referring to my presentation and, to my delight, informed the audience that the museum owned a copy of the *Illustrations of the Nests and Eggs of Birds of Ohio*. The book would be on display in the archives during the first break so that those interested could take a look at it.

Later, when the archives library was filled with admiring conference attendees carefully turning pages and examining details of the lithographs, the archivist confided that he was planning to include *Illustrations of the Nests and Eggs of Birds of Ohio* among the special volumes he pulled to show visiting royalty or heads of state, because of the beauty of its illustrations and the heartfelt story of the family behind its creation. I felt relieved and proud that Gennie's book was destined to be recognized by such a prestigious institution.

Many individuals and institutions contributed to this project. I am especially indebted to Leslie K. Overstreet of the Smithsonian Institution Libraries—she corresponded with me after the conference at UVA, helped me craft the research for my paper for the conference in London, accepted me as a Smithsonian Institution Behind-the-

Scenes Volunteer when I moved to DC to become the librarian for the National Endowment for the Arts, and responded to my suggestion of creating a web exhibit about the *Illustrations of the Nests and Eggs of Birds of Ohio* for their digital library.

It was there that Sara Bader, acquisitions editor at Princeton Architectural Press (PAP), discovered the story that she envisioned as a book. Sara provided guidance throughout the process, was an inexhaustible source of moral support and advice, and spent countless hours transcribing the field notes from volume two.

The Jones family's descendents, especially the Lloyd Jonnes family of Washington, DC, and the Nelson Jonnes family of Stillwater, Minnesota—both families use a variant spelling of the surname—contributed private reminiscences and cheerfully responded to my endless questions. Nelson's son Steven scoured the family archives and provided digital scans of photographs and documents; he also laboriously transcribed his great-grandfather's key to the eggs.

PAP editor Linda Lee then took up the reins and skillfully whittled down the field notes to their very essence, preserving Howard Jones's individual style and voice, while perfecting and polishing the material so that it would interface smoothly with the artistic vision that designer Bree Anne Apperley had for the book.

Throughout the years of my research, historian Wallace Higgins and his wife, Carol, of Circleville provided ceaseless encouragement and helped verify locations, dates, and details, drawing from their own vast knowledge of their hometown.

Finally, I am extremely grateful to the Cleveland Museum of Natural History for giving me the honor of caring for and studying their copy of the book and for funding the many research trips that were required to collect the historical materials that have coalesced into *America's Other Audubon*.

Gennie as a young woman.
Howard tipped this photograph into the front of his mother's copy of the
Illustrations of the Nests and Eggs of Birds of Ohio.

INTRODUCTION

I doubt if any other Family with our pecuniary means ever will raise for themselves such a Monument as "the [*sic*] *Birds of America*" is over their tomb!

—John James Audubon

John James Audubon was justly proud of his family's accomplishment. When he penned this sentiment to his son Victor, in 1833, he would never have imagined that forty-six years later a young woman would be so inspired by his work that she would personally begin creating a book that would become the monument over her family's tomb.

That young woman, Genevieve Estelle Jones—the cherished and only daughter of Dr. Nelson E. Jones and his wife, Virginia—was born on May 13, 1847. Genevieve (known by her friends and family as Gennie) was a joyful, inquisitive child who preferred to play outdoors. She and her brother, Howard, who was six years younger, grew up in Circleville, Ohio, a town adjacent to the Ohio and Erie Canal and surrounded by wetlands.

Gennie and Howard's father was a passionate amateur ornithologist who had studied medicine at the Cleveland Medical College under Jared Potter Kirtland, a physician, scientist, and naturalist who exchanged scientific specimens and corresponded with the leading personalities in the field of natural history in the United States and abroad. Kirtland had a tremendous influence on his medical students and also mentored a group of local young men from Cleveland's most prominent families. They met regularly in a two-room building to discuss advances in science and to study natural history specimens. The meeting space was so cluttered with stuffed bird and animal specimens that it was nicknamed "the Ark." The society's members were known as Arkites.[1]

Nelson shared his passion for natural history and for birds with his children. As a six-year-old, Gennie began accompanying her father when he visited his patients and continued to do so into adulthood. During those early buggy rides, Nelson taught her the basics of ornithology, and with the assistance of an English Cocker Spaniel named Archos, they searched for birds' nests and collected eggs to add to their natural history cabinet for further study.[2]

On one of these outings, Gennie found an intricate nest that neither Nelson nor Howard could identify. She searched in her father's extensive library to discover the bird that had built it, only to learn that no one had yet written a book on the nests and eggs of American birds. Gennie remarked that surely someone would have created a book to help people differentiate one nest from another. Howard casually offered to gather the nests and eggs for such a project if Gennie, who enjoyed painting and drawing, wanted to illustrate them. For many years, as Nelson, Gennie, and Howard furthered their study of American ornithology, the subject of the need for such a book came up during family conversations.

Virginia had absolutely no interest in the natural world. Nevertheless, she lovingly nurtured her family's avocations, only objecting when the singing of the hand-raised or rescued songbirds kept caged in her children's bedrooms grew so loud that it woke the neighbors at dawn. As the family aviary expanded to include larger birds—a Cooper's Hawk, an American Crow, a Turkey Vulture, a Belted Kingfisher, and two Screech Owls—it was relocated to the barn behind the house.

Gennie and Howard were homeschooled by their mother until they were of high-school age. Howard thought of himself as a bit antisocial, a mediocre and reluctant student who would have been perfectly content to spend his time roaming the woods alone. Gennie, on the other hand, excelled in schoolwork, especially mathematics, science, and languages, but she was an artist at heart. She was also a fine seamstress (she made all of her own clothes), penman, and china painter; an accomplished pianist and flutist; and a graceful dancer. She grew into a stately young woman, 5 feet 10½ inches tall, with dark brown hair and eyes.

When she graduated from high school in 1865, she continued her education at home, where she was tutored in French, Greek, and German—she also continued her musical studies. Reverend Samuel Hildeburn McMullin, her Greek tutor and a former college professor, considered her the most adept scholar he had ever taught. Her music teacher, Mr. Rosenfelt, eventually refused to accept money for lessons because her musical prowess had exceeded his own. Gennie was also an avid reader: her favorite novel was George Eliot's *Middlemarch* (1874). When she wasn't studying, practicing music, or reading, she took great delight in beating the local young men at checkers. And she loved to drive her little mare, Black Poney, into the countryside to study birds.

The Jones's library was the most frequently used room in the house and a popular place for spirited discussions among friends from the Circleville community, but the Jones family remained intensely tight-knit and formed few true intimacies outside their private little clan. "We derived our greatest pleasure from contact with each other," Howard reminisced.[3]

After Howard graduated from high school in 1871, he continued his studies at Hobart College in Geneva, New York, where Virginia's brother, Hamilton L. Smith, a professor of astronomy and physics, could keep a watchful eye on him. Hamilton (Uncle Ham) was a positive role model and a notable scientist, whose accomplishments include helping to build the largest telescope in the United States at the time (when he was a sixteen-year-old student at Yale University), running the Yale Observatory with his best friend, Ebenezer Porter Mason—the two conducted and published the first in-depth observations of interstellar clouds of gases (nebulae)—being elected president of the American Microscopical Society, and inventing the tintype camera that popularized photography in the United States.

Nelson and Virginia were reluctant to permit Howard to travel so far away from home. In an era when very large families were the norm—Virginia had ten siblings and Nelson had eight—the Joneses were understandably anxious and protective of their only two offspring. But they acknowledged that their son would need a vocation that would allow him to properly support a family of his own and hoped that Howard would choose a career in medicine, a field that required the kind of superior preparatory courses that Hobart offered.

When Nelson sent money to Howard to pay for his textbooks, Howard purchased duplicate copies to be sent home to Gennie, who studied his college curriculum independently. When he came home for visits, Howard found that his sister had surpassed him in his own areas of study. She had mastered chemistry, algebra, and calculus, he noted, and "got more out of the Greek and Latin poets and Herodotus" than he had derived with the guidance of experts.[4]

By nature Gennie was deeply sensitive and easily upset. She was noticeably more anxious during the Civil War, when her father served as an examining surgeon for the Union Army and received threatening letters from disgruntled inductees, or their families, and was shot at while driving his buggy at night. She began suffering from frequent, severe headaches, and her eyes bothered her when she attempted to read or sketch or paint.

During the period of Reconstruction that followed the war, which encompassed the years that Howard was away from home, Gennie suffered from outbreaks of acne rosacea, a skin disease in which blood vessels of the face enlarge, resulting in a flushed appearance. No one could pin down a specific medical cause. Although Howard asked his professors to suggest treatments and cures, and sent prescriptions home in his letters, none of these methods proved effective. Gennie became painfully self-conscious of her appearance.

Approaching thirty and still unmarried, exceptionally tall at the time for a woman, incredibly talented and bright but with so little in common with her peers, Gennie must have felt isolated and left out. "Everyone seems to be leaving town," Gennie lamented. "Sallie Gillis goes week after next to be gone 'ad infinitum.' Mollie has gone. Flora Fichardt expects to go soon & every one [sic] seems to be going to have a good time, I intend to stay home, & have a good time too, if such a thing can be had in Circleville."[5] Howard later recalled: "As I saw it then and remember it now, there seemed to be something lacking in her life that gave a touch of sadness to me at times, and I felt that her mother and father saw it but I do not remember that it was spoken of between us."[6]

There was one person outside of Gennie's immediate family who was not intimidated by her many talents and whose intellect and artistic sensibilities meshed with her own and "to whom she seemed to give her affections…and who seemed to be as fond of her as she was of him," as Howard described. Howard characterized Gennie's suitor—whose name sadly is lost to history—as a "fine looking gentlemanly fellow, with a wonderful memory. He was self-educated, but having traveled much and having a superior intelligence, he had acquired much pleasing learning." The man was ten years Gennie's senior and an exceptional musician and literary critic, but, unfortunately, as Howard explained, he was a periodical drunkard.[7]

Nelson and Virginia were fond of the man but objected to the relationship because of his drinking. Nelson firmly believed that alcohol should be used for medicinal purposes only; Virginia was an active member of the American Temperance Society, the local meetings of which were held in the Jones's home. Nelson requested a promise from the couple not to marry for one year, during which the suitor would remain sober. If he was successful, Nelson would grant him his blessing. After several failed attempts, Nelson reluctantly forbade the two from marrying. Gennie became indescribably despondent.

Gennie surely must have shared her feelings of sorrow and grief with her closest friend, Eliza Shulze. Perhaps it was Eliza's relatives with whom Gennie stayed in Pennsylvania, to experience a change of scenery and to come to terms with her disappointment. While she was there, she attended the Centennial International Exhibition in Philadelphia and saw some of the hand-colored engravings from Audubon's *The Birds of America* (1826–38). She was reminded that even Audubon had failed to chronicle a comprehensive number of bird eggs and nests. On the rare occasion a nest was included in one of Audubon's prints, the nest was more decorative than an element meant to convey scientific information.

When Gennie returned to Circleville, she had grown silent and withdrawn. Her suitor seldom visited, but when he did it was abundantly clear that they both remained deeply hurt. Something had to be done to raise Gennie's spirits. Nelson and Virginia urged Howard, who had completed his college education and was back in Circleville practicing medicine with his father, to encourage her to undertake the production of the book that had been incubating for years—the book illustrating the nests and eggs of American birds that was missing from ornithological literature. When Gennie had proposed the project in the past, Nelson had been hesitant because of the astronomical cost of creating such a lavishly illustrated book. But now he felt so personally responsible for her anguish because he had pressured her to break off her engagement that he was compelled to help her initiate a project of her very own, one that would engage her passion for art and nature, and distract her from her sadness.

Family and friends were encouraging and supportive. Howard again offered to gather the nests and eggs and to compose the field notes; Eliza agreed to assist with the drawing and coloring of the illustrations;

Reverend McMullin (who would later become Howard's father-in-law) volunteered to proofread the text and assure the accuracy of the Latin scientific names; and Nelson proposed to finance the project, expecting that it would eventually become self-supporting.

Gennie accepted the challenge and planned to illustrate the nests and eggs of all 320 species of American birds, but Nelson persuaded her to limit the number to the 130 species of birds that nested in Ohio.[8] (Most of these birds are common throughout the rest of the United States.) While Gennie and Eliza practiced sketching nests in the Jones's dining room—using a pair of calipers to take precise measurements and a magnifying glass to examine details—Nelson researched the procedure for publishing a book, corresponding with his friends in the ornithological community for advice and to find subscribers.

Nelson's business plan was to produce one hundred copies of Gennie's book, *Illustrations of the Nests and Eggs of Birds of Ohio*, which would be issued in approximately twenty-three parts and sold by subscription. Each part (three illustrations of nests and eggs with text) would cost $5.00 for the hand-painted version and $2.00 for the uncolored version. The nests and eggs would be drawn true to size, colored by hand with imported Winsor & Newton watercolors, and printed on Whatman's Hot-pressed Antiquarian paper—the same brand of imported paper that Audubon had used for his illustrations because it retained its bright white color indefinitely.

The Adolph Krebs Lithographic Company, a Cincinnati-based publisher, was hired to print the illustrations, and Krebs offered to instruct Gennie and Eliza in lithography through correspondences. The Robert Clarke Company, also of Cincinnati, would print the text. As the work in the dining room progressed, it quickly became apparent that the house was not a suitable workplace: gas lamps failed to provide adequate illumination, and the clutter of nests was turning the room into a "jungle."

So Nelson added a two-room upper story, with windows facing north and east, to the barn behind the family home. This studio (Gennie's private Ark) became the Office of the *Illustrations of the Nests and Eggs of Birds of Ohio*.

After Nelson secured twenty subscribers, among them some of the most celebrated ornithologists in the country, the work began in earnest. Gennie and Eliza drew illustrations in wax pencil on both sides of sixty-five-pound lithographic stones. Then Howard placed the stones into crates that were shipped eighty-nine miles to Cincinnati, where Krebs's artisans fixed the drawings with a solution of nitric acid, applied ink to the surface of the stones, and printed test proofs to determine the quality of the renderings. When errors were found, the ink was cleaned off and the stones were recreated and shipped back to Circleville for corrections. The first stones made several trips back and forth before the artists conquered the challenges of keeping the points on the wax crayons sharp and the edges of the line drawings crisp.

The three lithographs of part one were completed in 1878, and sample copies were sent out in December to ornithological publications for review. Gennie's and Eliza's artwork was widely praised as equal to—or even better than—Audubon's. Elliott Coues, the editor of the *Bulletin of Nuttall Ornithological Club* and one of the preeminent ornithologists of the period, wrote, "I had no idea that so sumptuous and elegant a publication was in preparation, and am pleased that what promises to be one of the great illustrated works on North American Ornithology should be prepared by women."[9] William Brewster, the founder and president of the American Ornithologists' Union, responded favorably: "The nest of the Wood Thrush is even more admirably delineated and is in its kind a perfect masterpiece. I find that my eyes dwell on it long and lovingly every time that I open the work and glance through its pages. Please accept my grateful thanks for part I of your beautiful work, and also my best wishes for the future prosperous continuance of a work that is too good to fail."[10]

Part one was mailed to the first subscribers during July of 1879. The response was so positive that the subscription list jumped to thirty-nine—now there were a total of thirty-four subscriptions for the hand-painted edition and five for the uncolored version—and included the names of former President Rutherford B. Hayes and then Harvard College student Theodore Roosevelt. Gennie and Eliza were overwhelmed by the task of hand coloring one hundred copies of each illustration for the proposed one hundred complete volumes (because it often took four days to complete just one nest), so they decided to color only fifty of the hundred printed and put the others aside to paint later. Nelson commissioned a specially constructed cabinet with twenty-four drawers to house the uncolored illustrations and sheets of text. Only one month after part one had been issued—with the future of the book project looking so promising—Gennie was struck with typhoid fever. She was violently ill for three weeks. During a lucid moment, she asked Howard to sit beside her on the bed. "I am going to die and if you and Lizzie want to you can go on with the book just as if I were alive. Mother will help you," she said.[11] He tried to rally her, reminding her of her dream of creating the book. The following day, Sunday, August 17, 1879, she died at the age of thirty-two. Gennie had completed only five illustrations for the book that was to have been her life's work.[12] Gennie's obituary, which was written by Lillie Darst, the editor of the *Circleville Democrat and Watchman* and one of her former classmates, closed with these words: "There is a pause in the busy pencil, the great Master saith to his pupil, 'Child, it is evenfall, get thee to rest.' For her there is a folding of hands, for the one who is left a duty sweet as a sacrament."[13]

Her family was paralyzed by grief and shock. In the Victorian tradition of mourning, the pendulum on the clock in the parlor was stopped at the moment of Gennie's death, and it stood still for many weeks.

Part two of Gennie's book could be mailed to subscribers on schedule because it was already finished, but the future of the project was unknown. After several weeks of deliberation, Virginia decided that she would complete her daughter's book as a way to honor and memorialize her. Although Eliza lost interest in the project in the absence of Gennie, she stayed in Circleville long enough to teach Virginia the lithographic technique. She sold her interest in the book's copyright to Nelson and moved to New York to attend art school. She eventually became a successful portrait painter and art teacher.

Gennie's former suitor was so overcome with sorrow that he later committed suicide by overdosing on morphine. "He often spoke to me about Genevieve and lamented her death," Howard wrote. "I always thought he felt somewhat to blame."[14]

Gennie's book became the Jones family's transitional object, a physical entity with which they could distract themselves from their heartache and into which they could invest their passion and energy. Virginia poured all the love she could no longer give to her daughter into illustrating the nests and eggs. Virginia had never drawn or painted anything that required scientific accuracy before. Examples of her china painting and illustrations in a book she created for her husband in 1862 reveal a simplistic depiction of flowers and scenery that makes no attempt to convey the underlying structures and systems. Despite her grief, she struggled with overcoming her casual artistic style and transformed herself into a scientific observer. Analysis and intellectual rigor were essential, because an artist does not draw what she sees, she draws what she understands. Miraculously, Virginia was soon producing lithographs that were every bit as lovely, exacting, and accurate as her daughter's.

But it was impossible for a single person to hand color fifty copies of every illustration. Virginia drew each new image on the lithographic stones and colored a master plate for colorists to follow. Two local girls were hired to assist. Kate Gephart, the lesser skilled, colored the less important parts of each composition, and Nellie Jacob colored the patterns on the eggs. Virginia also hired Josephine Klippart, the artist based in Columbus, Ohio, who later founded the Ohio Watercolor Society, to help color the nests themselves. Even Josephine's mother assisted for a short period of time. Eventually, Howard assumed responsibility for drawing the eggs.

With three assistants being paid from $1.00 to $3.00 for each illustration they painted, the subscription installment payment of $5.00 for one hand-colored part—three illustrations with text—fell significantly short of covering publication expenses. But Nelson hoped that when the entire book was completed and had established a reputation, he could sell bound copies for a significant sum.

The quarterly installments of the publication were issued on time for two years until Virginia and Howard were both also stricken with typhoid fever. They recovered, but Howard suffered heart damage and Virginia's eyes were permanently weakened. Howard was unable to practice medicine for a year, but on his better days he continued to ride into the countryside to gather nests and eggs so that work on the book could proceed. And despite suffering severe eye pain and strain, Virginia persevered with her labor of love.

Gennie's memorial book was completed in 1886 and her dream of filling the gap in ornithological literature had been realized, but the victory was bittersweet.[15] To bring closure to their mourning, Nelson had Virginia's copy bound in two volumes in full red morocco leather by a Chicago bindery. These volumes were loaned to potential customers as a sample to review and tempted some buyers, but few people could afford the luxurious, folio-sized book with hand-colored illustrations.

Virginia entered her copy in the Women's Building Library exhibit in the World's Columbian Exposition of 1893, in Chicago, where it won a bronze medal. When Caroline Harwood Garland inquired, while writing a review for the *Library Journal*, how Virginia had the patience to complete it, Virginia responded, "I did it in memory of my daughter. She had just begun the work when she died. So for her sake I made it as perfect as possible."[16]

Nelson had two-volume copies of the work bound in red morocco and offered them for sale through various book dealers, both domestically and internationally. About fourteen sets of the work were sold this way but never for a sum that came close to offsetting the production costs. Nelson spent his entire retirement savings, $25,000, financing the project. Virginia was temporarily blind for two years from the effects of the typhoid fever and the long hours of straining her eyes to draw the nests.

In spite of the extraordinary financial and physical costs, neither parent was ever heard to complain. They both felt thankful that they had the resources to see the project through and considered their collective work on the book the most significant accomplishment of their lives. Nelson never recovered from his daughter's death. He remained a pension examiner for the United States Army, but gave up his medical practice and spent much of his time alone in the woods.

In truth, Circleville had not been Nelson's first choice for a place to raise his family. During his engagement to Virginia, he had traveled to Guttenberg, Iowa, to set up his first medical practice on the new western frontier and made close friends who fully expected their doctor to return and bring Mrs. Jones with him. But Virginia's father, Cleveland millionaire Anson Smith, had other plans for his beautiful daughter. How many times did Nelson regret bringing his children to a town that was closer to their grandparents but notorious for its outbreaks of typhoid fever?

After the deaths of Nelson (1901) and Virginia (1906), Howard locked the doors to the studio of the Office of the *Illustrations of the Nests and Eggs of Birds of Ohio*. The doors remained sealed for thirty-two years. The grandchildren, who grew up hearing about the book, were fiercely curious about the secret workroom. The mystery became too much for grandson Nelson III, who at the age of twelve sawed the hinges off the doors with his friend Sam Chambers to gain access to the forbidden space. Grandson Nelson related in 1998 that at the time, "the feeling of excitement was intense, but it could not begin to compare to the intensity of the retribution that followed."[17] Howard always remained deeply sentimental about the period of time the family had spent together working on their project.

Over the years Howard received occasional inquiries about the book. In 1924 the Arthur H. Clark Company, a Cleveland-based business-book publisher, as well as a buyer and seller of rare books, offered to purchase several copies of the book to bind for resale. The uncolored sets of illustrations and pages of text that had been stored in the twenty-four-drawer chest were bound into fourteen two-volume sets, with one hand-colored illustration as each volume's frontispiece. These volumes can be easily distinguished from the original subscription copies because they were all bound with green half morocco spines and green cloth boards. The Clark Company sold some of these sets, and others were marketed by the Anderson Gallery in New York, but only a few were sold.

Perhaps it was grandson Nelson's intrusion into the barn that prompted Howard to search for a suitable home for his mother's copy so that it would be preserved safely. An unidentified Cleveland woman purchased it from the Arthur H. Clark Company in 1924. Many years later the volumes were donated to the Cleveland Museum of Natural History by Dr. N. L. Siplock, a veterinarian from Chesterland, Ohio.

Howard spent the rest of his life trying to market remaining copies of Gennie's book. In the end many were given to his children and grandchildren. He never stopped believing that *Illustrations of the Nests and Eggs of Birds of Ohio* would one day be considered priceless. (The Cleveland Museum's copy was appraised at $80,000 in 1998; another copy of the work sold for $48,000 in 2010.) His last act in 1945, at the age of ninety-two, was to ask his daughter and his secretary to prop him up in bed so that he could sign over ownership of the five copies he had left to his daughter Eleanor.

The work Genevieve initiated broke new ground in the field of natural history illustration. When members of the American Ornithologists' Union gathered on April 20, 1917, to collectively celebrate the seventieth birthdays of members who had been born in 1847, the names of seven individuals were noted who had not lived long enough to reach that milestone but had still "left their names indelibly impressed on the records of ornithology." Miss Genevieve Estelle Jones was listed among them.

Of the proposed one hundred volumes, only ninety copies of Gennie's book were actually completed; fifty-three of those were hand-colored.[18] Currently, only twenty-six complete hand-colored copies and eight uncolored, or incomplete, copies have been located in the United States, France, Germany, and the United Kingdom, making Gennie's book exceedingly rare and virtually unknown.

Few people have had the opportunity to experience this nineteenth-century American masterpiece or to hear the unforgettable family story connected with its creation. It is an honor to share these magnificent lithographs on the following pages and to make this work readily available for the very first time.

INTRODUCTION

NOTES

The epigraph to the introduction is drawn from a letter from John James Audubon to his son Victor, December 21, 1833, the American Philosophical Society Archives, Philadelphia, PA.

1. The Ark was an informal gathering place for the Cleveland intellectuals who later established many of the city's cultural institutions: the Cleveland Museum of Natural History, the Cleveland Library Association, Case Western Reserve University, the Western Reserve Historical Society, the Cleveland Museum of Art, and Severance Hall (home of the Cleveland Orchestra).

2. In the nineteenth century it was common for amateur naturalists to collect bird nests and eggs and to store them in a wooden cabinet for scientific study. Today, because of the drastic decline in the number of migratory birds, it is illegal to disturb nesting birds or to remove eggs or nests from the wild.

3. Howard Jones, "Personal Reminiscences" (unpublished manuscript, 1931), Jonnes family archives, Springfield, VA.

4. Howard Jones, "Biography of Genevieve Estelle Jones" (unpublished manuscript, 1923), Jonnes family archives.

5. Gennie Jones, letter to Howard Jones at Hobart College, June 27, 1872, Jonnes family archives.

6. Howard Jones, "Biography of Genevieve Estelle Jones" (unpublished manuscript, 1931), Jonnes family archives.

7. Ibid.

8. In the end only 129 birds were represented because neither the nest nor eggs of the Cerulean Warbler could be found.

9. Elliott Coues, letter to Genevieve Jones and Eliza Shulze, December 14, 1878, Howard Jones Collection, Ohio Historical Society, Columbus, OH. The Nuttall Ornithological Club, founded in 1873 and named after Thomas Nuttall—an Englishman who became curator of the botanical gardens at Harvard University and published his *Manual of the Ornithology of the United States and of Canada* (1832 and 1834)— was the first ornithological organization founded in the United States.

10. William Brewster, letter to Genevieve Jones and Eliza Shulze, December 15, 1878, Howard Jones Collection, Ohio Historical Society, Columbus, OH.

Eliza's depiction of the Black-billed Cuckoo's nest was the only drawing that drew mildly negative criticism because of the artistic way she depicted the eggs dangling by a thread. The lithographs for subsequent parts showed the eggs at the bottom of the page and illustrated the smallest possible size of an egg, the average size, and the largest size.

11. Jones, "Biography of Genevieve Estelle Jones," 1931.

12. Gennie completed one of the three illustrations in part one (plate 2) and two in part two (plates 4 and 6). The rest were for later parts.

13. "Obituary," *Circleville Democrat and Watchman*, August 1879.

14. Jones, "Biography of Genevieve Estelle Jones," 1931.

15. It took eight years to draw and print the one hundred copies of each of the sixty-eight illustrations.

16. Virginia Jones, interview by Caroline Harwood Garland, "Some of the Libraries at the Exposition," *Library Journal* 18 (August 1893): 284–88.

17. Nelson Jonnes III, as related to Joy Kiser during his visit to the Cleveland Museum of Natural History, September 19, 1998.

18. Not all one hundred copies of each illustration were without errors in printing or accidents in painting, so one hundred copies of the book could not be put together. Odd plates were sold separately by Howard later (he colored them himself) for financial reasons.

Howard as a young man with his dog, Greek

PLATES

PLATE I.

ICTERUS BALTIMORE—Baltimore Oriole

Icterus galbula—Baltimore Oriole

Illustrated by Eliza Shulze

The nest figured was taken from the branches of an elm that stands by the sidewalk of a village street. It is composed principally of strings and fibers of flax, many of which are more than thirty inches in length; a few horsehairs are woven in near the mouth. Oviposition was begun the day following its completion. Only one of the eggs figured was taken from this set.

The depth and beauty of a nest, therefore, seems to depend more upon the materials at hand, the experience, genius, and hurry of the workers, than upon any other circumstances, each pair of birds shaping their home after their own ideas.

Pl. I.
ICTERUS BALTIMORE.
BALTIMORE ORIOLE.

PLATE II.

TURDUS MUSTELINUS—Wood Thrush

Hylocichla mustelina—Wood Thrush

Illustrated by Genevieve Jones

The same home is often occupied by the Wood Thrush for a series of years, the annual repairs consisting either of a new plastering and lining, or the latter alone. One nest in the authors' collection shows four distinct yearly additions. The whole was stoutly placed in a perpendicular fork, which enabled it to resist so well the wear and tear of the seasons. The nest was taken from a haw tree in a damp wood without much undergrowth. The light, fluffy leaves of the foundation, the mossy branches and emerald foliage, the boggy earth and rank grass beneath, together formed a picture beautiful and rustic, a fitting symbol of the quiet wood, the drear repose in which this brilliant songster so much delights.

Though the Wood Thrush is naturally shy, she rarely abandons her nest on account of intrusion; being repeatedly driven from it, she as often returns as soon as the danger is past.

Pl. II.
TURDUS MUSTELINUS.
WOOD THRUSH.

PLATE III.

COCCYZUS ERYTHROPHTHALMUS—Black-billed Cuckoo

Coccyzus erythrophthalmus—Black-billed Cuckoo

Illustrated by Eliza Shulze

The nest figured was taken from a thicket overgrown with climbing vines, in a low piece of woods near the Scioto River, Pickaway County. It was placed about seven feet from the ground, supported by the dead branches of a thorn tree, together with the stems of ivy which climbed about the tree. It contained four eggs. Its foundation is constructed of thorns and slender twigs from three to eight inches in length; upon this is a superstructure of layer upon layer of catkins of the oak, occasionally a slender twig, with small pieces of dried leaves and lichens. The lining consists of fine round stems of weeds and small tendrils, together with catkins that compose the bulk of the nest. The nest is rather difficult to find, owing to it being built in dense foliage. It is well known that the foreign cuckoos are parasites, and, like the Cowbird, deposit their eggs in the nests of other birds, leaving them to be reared by their foster-mother. The American cuckoos are occasionally guilty of the same misdemeanor.

The bird is shy, and shows but little attachment to her nest and eggs, and rarely complains when robbed. Authorities state that it plunders the nests of other birds, after the habit of the Blue Jay, and even devours the young.

Pl. III.
COCCYZUS ERYTHROPHTHALMUS.
BLACK-BILLED CUCKOO.

PLATE IV.

CYANOSPIZA CYANEA—Indigo Bird

Passerina cyanea—Indigo Bunting

Illustrated by Genevieve Jones

The nest was taken from an elder bush. The foundation consists of pieces of leaves and corn husks, mixed with rootlets, weed stems, and grasses; the superstructure is similar but with finer rootlets about the rim. The lining is composed of almost equal proportions of split grasses, fine bits of roller-grass, and black horsehairs. Cobwebs are attached at irregular distances to the exterior and seem to be used more for ornament than for any additional strength they may give to the structure.

His spirited warblings can be heard along the public roads and by-ways. From the humblest bush to the topmost branch of the forest tree, the brilliantly plumed male pours forth his melodies, seeming to make of the summer months one continual round of holidays.

Pl. IV.
CYANOSPIZA CYANEA.
INDIGO BIRD.

PLATE V.

AGELAEUS PHOENICEUS—Red-winged Blackbird

Agelaius phoeniceus—Red-winged Blackbird

Illustrated by Eliza Shulze

When built in reeds, the structure is woven between a number of blades, as figured in the plate, and often within a few inches of the surrounding water. The nest illustrated was taken from a swamp. It is composed principally of dried grasses and strips of leaves, lined with round grass and a few black horse hairs. The eggs figured were selected from a large number.

Pl. V.
AGELÆUS PHŒNICEUS.
RED-WINGED BLACKBIRD.

PLATE VI.

TYRANNUS CAROLINENSIS—Kingbird (a.k.a. Beebird)

Tyrannus tyrannus—Eastern Kingbird

Illustrated by Genevieve Jones

The nest represented in the drawing was taken from a sycamore growing on the bank of the canal. The foundation is composed of dried grasses, weed stems and fibers, straws, and sticks; the superstructure is of similar but finer and better selected material, well plastered within, and ornamented without with pods from the wild cucumber vine. The lining is of round grass, horsehairs, feathers, and wool.

Pl. VI.
TYRANNUS CAROLINENSIS.
KINGBIRD.

PLATE VII.

QUISCALUS PURPUREUS var. AENEUS, RIDGWAY—Crow Blackbird (a.k.a. Bronzed Grackle)

Quiscalus quisicaula—Common Grackle

Illustrated by Eliza Shulze

The nest illustrated was taken from a piece of wet grassland. The foundation and superstructure consist of coarse grasses and the stalks of small weeds, those on the inside of the superstructure being well smeared with mud before they were placed in position: the plaster of mud extends to the rim, and is entirely covered by the lining of round grasses.

Ornithological writers seem to agree that the Crow Blackbird is a cowardly thief, and a habitual plunderer of the nests of other birds.

Pl. VII.
QUISCALUS PURPUREUS var ÆNEUS, Rdgw.
CROW BLACKBIRD.

PLATE VIII.

TURDUS MIGRATORIUS—Robin

Turdus migratorius—American Robin

Illustrated by Eliza Shulze

The nest illustrated was taken from a small elm tree growing in a field near a road. The foundation contains but little material, this consists of weed stems and mud; the superstructure is composed of finer weed stems, fibers, grasses, a few chicken feathers, and the usual plaster of mud; the lining is of blades of grass, which are very unevenly distributed. The mother bird is, by close observers, said to build the nest unassisted by her mate. The male may now and then bring a stick or straw, but she does not permit him to take an active part either as architect or builder.

PLATE IX.

COLLURIO LUDOVICIANUS—Loggerhead Shrike
Lanius ludovicianus—Loggerhead Shrike
Illustrated by Virginia Jones

The old birds are much attached to place, and rarely go far away from the spot selected. Notwithstanding this apparent attachment to place, they exhibit no such feeling in regard to their nest; they are easily driven from it while setting, and seldom make any attempt at defense, but will fly to some neighboring tree and silently see the eggs or even the young taken away without manifesting the least concern. When the nest is robbed they immediately set to work to replace it, building in the same tree or in one near by.

The nest illustrated was taken from a thorn tree standing on the bank of a canal; it contained six eggs. The eggs illustrated are from three different sets; they represent the extremes and average, both in size and color.

It is singular that it has so few acquaintances, as its habits are perhaps more interesting than those of any of our other birds.

Pl. IX.
COLLURIO LUDOVICIANUS.
LOGGERHEAD SHRIKE.

PLATE X.

SAYORNIS FUSCUS—Pewit Flycatcher

Sayornis phoebe—Eastern Phoebe

Illustrated by Genevieve Jones

Attachment to the nesting locality is strong in the Phoebe. Throughout their lives, if circumstances are favorable, the same pair will return every spring to their first nesting spot, and sometimes even bring with them their offspring, to build in the immediate neighborhood of their birthplace. This habit endears them to the country people—in fact, to all who are acquainted with the bird—and "the nest on the porch pillar" is as studiously guarded as if an unfailing omen of good luck.

This nest was built early in May against an inch plank, used as a brace between the timbers of a wooden culvert, about four feet above the surface of the run. It contained five fresh eggs. The road passing over the bridge was much traveled, but the clatter of horses' hoofs and rattle of wagons, though loud and frightful to a person beneath, did not seem to annoy the birds, which, judging from the various marks of former nests, had occupied the place for a number of years.

The tedium of sitting on the nest is perhaps somewhat lightened by the cool, contented notes—pee-wee, pee-wee—which her mate encouragingly utters at short intervals throughout the summer days.

Pl. X.
SAYORNIS FUSCUS.
PEWIT FLYCATCHER.

PLATE XI.

THRYOTHORUS LUDOVICIANUS—Great Carolina Wren

Thryothorus ludovicianus—Carolina Wren

Illustrated by Eliza Shulze

Although this wren appears shy and fond of secluded little nooks, it has so much curiosity, and such a manifest liking for the works and company of man, and the protection which his presence affords, that it is content to build beside the very door of his house if a foot of space is given up for its sole occupancy.

The nest when found contained six eggs nearly hatched. It was built in a box nailed against the inside of an old barn and used only a short time before as a hen's nest. When taken possession of by the wren, the box was nearly full of straw and grass. In this, near one corner, a cavity was made to receive the nest. The illustration shows the nest as it was lifted from the cavity, some of the grasses still hanging to it. The materials used in its construction included pieces of snakeskin.

It is possessor of an exceedingly attractive voice, and being indefatigable in its efforts to be heard, is well known and much admired.

PL. XI.
THRYOTHORUS LUDOVICIANUS.
GREAT CAROLINA WREN.

PLATE XII.

SIALIA SIALIS—Eastern Bluebird

Sialia sialis—Eastern Bluebird

Illustrated by Eliza Shulze

I have repeatedly known the Eastern Bluebird to attempt to drive other birds from their homes, and generally the attempt is successful. The Red-headed Woodpecker is a frequent victim to this scheme. Having labored hard to excavate a suitable habitation, and about ready to begin the cares of housekeeping, they are often set upon by a pair of bluebirds, and so persistent is the attack that the woodpeckers, perhaps afraid more blood will be spilled upon their already scarlet heads, disgracefully retreat.

The nest was built in an old black walnut stump in a wheat field. The part containing the nest was sawed-off below and split open so as to give a clear side view of the structure, which was composed of blades of grass and contained five eggs. The entrance to the cavity was from above, and was distant from the ground about two feet.

Pl. XII.
SIALIA SIALIS.
EASTERN BLUEBIRD.

PLATE XIII.

HIRUNDO ERYTHROGASTER, BODDAERT—Barn Swallow

Hirundo rustica—Barn Swallow

Illustrated by Eliza Shulze

The nest was built against a rafter in an old scale house. The eggs figured show the average and two extremes in size and markings most commonly met with.

Pl. XIII.
HIRUNDO ERYTHROGASTER, Bodd.
BARN SWALLOW.

PLATE XIV.

COCCYZUS AMERICANUS—Yellow-billed Cuckoo (a.k.a. Rain Crow, Rain Dove)
Coccyzus americanus—Yellow-billed Cuckoo
Illustrated by Eliza Shulze

The nest illustrated was taken from a black haw tree. The branches upon which the nest rested were inclined at an angle of forty degrees. The plate shows the branches in a perpendicular position, the nest being thus inclined sufficiently to give a view of the upper surface. The materials of construction are sticks and catkins of the oak. The dried leaves belong to the dead branch, which is lodged in the fork.

The character of the Yellow-billed Cuckoo is not above suspicion. In fact it was long-ago convicted of theft and murder, though perhaps not quite so bloodthirsty as the Blue Jay.

Pl. XIV.
COCCYZUS AMERICANUS.
YELLOW-BILLED CUCKOO.

PLATE XV.

DENDROECA AESTIVA—Summer Warbler
Dendroica petechia—Yellow Warbler
Illustrated by Genevieve Jones

The nest was taken from a small elm on the bank of a river. The nest of the Summer Warbler has always been a subject of admiration. It represents strength, comfort, beauty, everything necessary for a cozy summer home; so compact is it, that it may be seen firmly attached to its supports after the frosts and winds of fall have stripped the foliage from the trees, and even the rains, snows, and gales of severe winter often fail to dislodge it.

Though exceedingly friendly and familiar, {the Summer Warblers are very} watchful and solicitous, and seldom go far from home during the nesting season. When robbed by man they exhibit much feeling, and scold incessantly the thief they are too tiny to attack.

Pl. XV.
DENDRŒCA ÆSTIVA.
SUMMER WARBLER.

PLATE XVI.

SPIZELLA PUSILLA—Field Sparrow

Spizella pusilla—Field Sparrow

Illustrated by Virginia Jones

When the female is sitting upon a nest in the bushes and is quietly approached, she will permit a close inspection of her home without showing any fear, turning her head in a quizzical way and with her bright black eye carefully scanning the visitor from crown to foot.

The illustration was made from a nest taken from a wild rosebush. The foundation consists of weed stalks and a few straws; the superstructure of finer weed stems, fibers, and split grasses; the lining of horsehair and roller grass.

The Field Sparrow is retiring in its habits, and therefore has few acquaintances except among ornithologists.

PLATE XVII.

MIMUS CAROLINENSIS—Catbird

Dumetella carolinensis—Gray Catbird

Illustrated by Virginia Jones

The cry of the bird is so like the animal after which it is named, that the association is not at all calculated to give it character. For of all our singing birds, save one, there is none that can excel him in variety and combination of notes, though it must be admitted that they are at times very harsh and unpleasant.
A particular catbird, which built for several seasons in the yard of a friend, so excelled as a vocalist and mimic that he attracted the attention and admiration of the whole neighborhood. At intervals throughout the day, from a favorite perch upon a pear tree, he would drop his tail and wings, loosen his feathers until they seemed to stand almost on end, and assuming a comical, semiquizzical look, pour forth volumes of as pure notes as ever came from a feathery throat. He commanded the attention of a large audience, which he would first please, then astonish, then disappoint, then enrapture, then amuse, and finally, just as twilight was fading into night, as if it was a fitting tailpiece to his opéra-bouffe, he would convulse his hearers with laughter by mimicking the crow of a young Cochin rooster confined in a coop nearby.

The foundation of this nest is composed of twigs of oak, weed stems, and slender pieces of grapevine. The superstructure consists largely of grapevine bark; the lining is of rootlets.

PLATE XVIII.

ORTYX VIRGINIANUS—Quail—Bob-White

Colinus virginianus—Northern Bobwhite

Illustrated by Virginia Jones

Original text by Nelson Jones

The Quail–Bob-White is really a bird of civilization. He flourishes best near the abodes of man. The cultivation of the soil and settlement of the country increase their number seemingly by lessening their dangers and giving an easy mode of subsisting. With no friend but agriculture, with no protection but fields of grass and grain, they become abundant in spite of the hawk, the owl, the crow, the blue jay, the opossum, the raccoon, the polecat, the weasel, the fox, the Norway rat, the snake, the dog, the cat, the mowing machine, the sportsman, the trapper, the heavy summer rains, and the winter snows. Quail are not strictly granivorous in their notions of diet. As an insect exterminator is only one of many instances illustrating the practical usefulness of these birds to the farmer.

They are always amiable and gentle in their family relations, and rarely domineering or vindictive toward their friendly associates. They are cowardly towards their enemies; and while in coveys, seem to maintain a sense of security by keeping close together; and so strong is this feeling that wounded birds, unable to fly, will follow after their companions on foot, as long as able to go. When paired, the two are constant companions, ever watchful over the welfare of each other. They share equally the duties and responsibilities of wedded life, and from the birth of the first offspring to their settlement in the world, as faithful father and mother, are unceasing protectors and providers for the family.

The nest was built near the remaining root of an old stump surrounded with grass and a few stalks of clover. The eggs were completely concealed by the covering which the grass afforded, but in making the drawing this protection was separated sufficiently to show the nest and eggs. The nest is composed of dead grass, dry leaves, and weed stems.

When mating has taken place, it is known at once by the demonstrations of the male, who gives to the whole neighborhood due notice of his domestic intentions by frequent repetitions at short intervals, of his cheerful and well-known notes—*Bob-White, Bob-White*.

Pl. XVIII.

ORTYX VIRGINIANUS.
QUAIL.

PLATE XIX.

Fig. 1. EMPIDONAX ACADICUS—Acadian Flycatcher
Empidonax virescens—Acadian Flycatcher
Illustrated by Eliza Shulze

When the Acadian Flycatcher is approached while sitting, she will permit the hand within a few inches of her nest before flying. If driven off, she will alight on some low limb nearby, and sometimes will utter, in measured succession, her faint, mellow cry; but generally she silently watches the intruder. If the nest contains young, she may perhaps show more concern, but she never blusters or loses her slow, dignified air. The male seems to be entirely free from any anxiety or concern about the family, let happen what may. The young leave the nest the thirteenth or fourteenth day after they are hatched.

    The nest illustrated was taken from a black haw tree.

Fig. 2. CONTOPUS VIRENS—Wood Peewee
Contopus virens—Eastern Wood-Pewee
Illustrated by Eliza Shulze

The nest of the Wood Peewee is difficult to find, owing to its small size, lichen-covered exterior, and obscure position. Even when situated in a conspicuous place, upon a dead branch, it is easily mistaken for a lichen-covered excrescence so common upon the trees which the Wood Peewee frequents. When the nest is disturbed the owners often show considerable courage, but different individuals are as variable in valor as are individuals of the human family. One pair may fight for their nest, another only scold, and still another may silently see home and eggs demolished or carried away, without uttering the least protest. The Wood Peewees are fond of quiet and solitude, but they do not habitually resort to the dense woods.

Pl. XIX Fig. 1.
EMPIDONAX ACADICUS.
ACADIAN FLYCATCHER.

Fig 2.
CONTOPUS VIRENS.
WOOD PEWEE.

PLATE XX.

ICTERIA VIRENS—Yellow-breasted Chat

Icteria virens—Yellow-breasted Chat

Illustrated by Virginia Jones

The nest of the Chat is very easily found, as the male bird always betrays the secret by his continual song. When undisturbed, he faithfully keeps watch over his property; on the approach of danger he at once sounds an alarm note, and then endeavors to persuade the intruder to follow him right to the nest, being careful however to go in an opposite direction. If not successful in his attempts to mislead, he commences a terrible tirade of abuse.

This is the male Yellow-breasted Chat. The clownish actions and peculiar whistles are his best endeavors to please his chosen partner, who, concealed in the thick foliage, admiringly watches his queer antics.

Pl. XX.
ICTERIA VIRENS,
YELLOW-BREASTED CHAT.

PLATE XXI.

GEOTHLYPIS TRICHAS—Maryland Yellow-throat

Geothlypis trichas—Common Yellowthroat

Illustrated by Virginia Jones

The Maryland Yellow-throat is the most terrestrial of any of the family. Much of their time is spent among grass, weeds, and low bushes; rarely they resort to the treetops, and then to utter for a few minutes only their sharp and shrill notes. In their domestic relations they are very model birds. The male assists the female in collecting the materials for the nest, and he seems to take the greatest interest in all affairs of the home. During the period of incubation he stays close by the nest, and accompanies his partner when she leaves for food. They guard their treasure with the greatest solicitude, resorting to various strategies at the approach of danger to draw attention from their domicile. But when these means fail, and the nest is about to be robbed, they sometimes show a remarkable degree of valor.

The nest when found contained four fresh eggs. It was built among the perpendicular stalks of a clump of goldenrod, growing along a little used river-road. A recent freshet had drifted leaves, broken stems, and rotten wood against the old stalks of the plant, two of which, bent and broken, are shown in the illustration. Upon this debris the bottom of the nest rested, while all about it long blades of grass and various weeds were forcing their way through the covering of drift.

Pl. XXI.
GEOTHLYPIS TRICHAS,
MARYLAND YELLOW-THROAT.

PLATE XXII.

CARDINALIS VIRGINIANUS—Cardinal Redbird
Cardinalis cardinalis—Northern Cardinal
Illustrated by Virginia Jones

The Cardinal Redbirds, in the winter, sometimes assemble in small flocks, and remain in thickets near by a suitable food supply. They are very fond of corn, which they readily peck from the ear with their stout bills. Being delightful songsters in captivity, the country lads set box traps with a figure four, and bait them with corn.

At the sight of man, the female redbird sits upon her eggs closely; if driven off, she flies silently away, and will suffer her nest to be robbed without a cry. But when the young are hatched, she becomes much bolder, and will defend them to the last. After they are large enough to leave the nest, the male seems to take especial interest in them. When one of the young is caught, both parents will follow the captor long distances. The male is really a bold bird. When wounded, he scratches and pecks the hand that holds him, and exhibits a bravery and muscular strength that one would little suspect in so small a body.

The nest was taken from a low branch of a young haw tree.

PLATE XXIII.

Fig. 1. VIREO GILVUS—Warbling Vireo
Vireo gilvus—Warbling Vireo
Illustrated by Virginia Jones

The song of the Warbling Vireo may be heard in the neighborhood of the nest almost any hour of the day. The male, as he moves from branch to branch, peering now for an insect on a leaf, now on a twig, gives forth a sweet, flutelike melody, in striking contrast to the rattle of wagons, clatter of feet, and hum of busy voices in the street beneath. While, in the country, where all is quiet, the music charms the listener, and holds him a willing captive, as he endeavors to translate into English the words set to the music of the busy little bird.

The nest was taken from a silver poplar standing beside a country road. It contained four fresh eggs. The foundation of this nest is composed of flaxen fibers and grasses; the superstructure of fibers, grasses, bits of decayed weeds, and a downy substance from the poplar; the lining is made entirely of roller grass.

Fig. 2. VIREO OLIVACEUS—Red-eyed Vireo
Vireo olivaceus—Red-eyed Vireo
Illustrated by Virginia Jones

The nest was taken from the extremity of an oak branch, seven feet from the ground. The exterior is composed of pieces of hornets' nests, strips of inner bark of trees and plants, shreds of the inner bark of the wild grapevine, and bits of web. The hornet paper is bound tightly with flaxen shreds, frequently a stitch is taken in it, as shown in the large piece in front. The interior is composed entirely of long shreds of the inner bark of the grapevine.

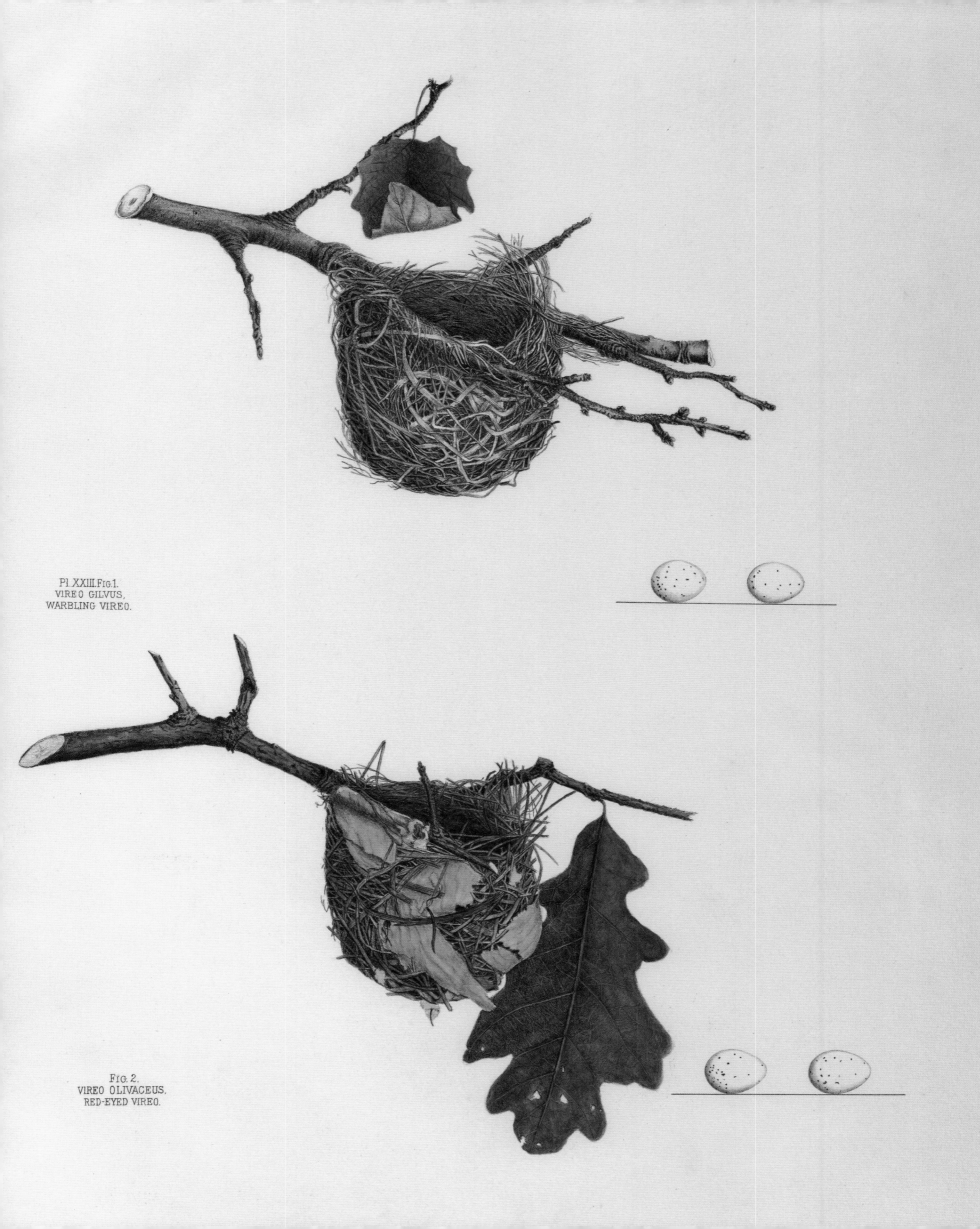

Pl. XXIII. Fig. 1.
VIREO GILVUS,
WARBLING VIREO.

Fig. 2.
VIREO OLIVACEUS.
RED-EYED VIREO.

PLATE XXIV.

ZENAEDURA CAROLINENSIS—Carolina Dove (a.k.a. Turtle Dove)

Zenaida macroura—Mourning Dove

Illustrated by Virginia Jones

During incubation the male Dove is very attentive to his partner; he often brings her water and food, which he feeds to her after the manner of the family, that is by regurgitation. When the young are hatched both parents supply food, but as soon as they are large enough to fly, the male takes them in charge and the female busies herself about the cares of another brood.

The nest was selected on account of the simplicity of its surroundings. It is a compact and elaborate structure, but no more so than is necessary for security. The position in which it is placed requires more material and better workmanship than if it had been situated upon a large limb. It is composed of twigs, roots, weed stems, and straws; the upper surface is made up of the same but finer material than the base.

The Turtle Dove is an exceedingly hardy bird; swift on the wing, well clothed with an abundance of compact feathers, and very tenacious of life, they brave {the} coldest winters.

PLATE XXV.

Fig. 1. TROCHILUS COLUBRIS—Ruby-throated Hummingbird
Archilochus colubris—Ruby-throated Hummingbird
Illustrated by Virginia Jones

The Ruby-Throat Hummingbird's nest is very difficult to find, even when the actions of the birds designate the tree on which it is built. When the locality in which the nest is placed is approached, both birds may attack the intruder in the most savage manner; they never actually strike, but they dart at the trespasser with such velocity that nothing can be seen but a hazy streak, while their buzzing wings and squealing voice indicate their anger. About the time they seem to have given up the attack and deserted the place, back they come with such suddenness as to startle any but the strongest nerves.

The domestic life of the hummingbird is a model in every respect, and in strict harmony with the beautiful little home they occupy. In confinement the hummingbird soon becomes tame but always at a loss of health and spirits. In 1875 one came into my room through an open window and was captured without injury in a butterfly net. The little fellow was imprisoned. Here he remained until the following winter, when he died, apparently of a broken heart.

The nest was taken from the limb of an apple tree. It contained two fresh eggs. It is a beautiful specimen of hummingbird architecture.

Fig. 2. POLIOPTILA CAERULEA—Blue-gray Gnatcatcher
Polioptila caerulea—Blue-gray Gnatcatcher
Illustrated by Virginia Jones

It has been suggested that this nest is covered with lichens so that it may appear like a natural woody excrescence, and by deluding enemies the safety of its contents is greatly increased. This may be the fact, but I receive the statement with doubt. The lichens and web make such a secure sheath about the walls, that these nests owe much of their strength and firmness to them. I can conceive of nothing better calculated to preserve the shape, to keep the walls dry, and at the same time give strength and lightness, than a lichen covering as found upon this nest, and that of the hummingbird.

The nest was taken from an oak tree. It contained, at the time, five fresh eggs. It was about twelve feet from the ground, and six feet from the tree trunk. The walls are composed of very fine fibers and shreds, compactly interwoven with little rolls of white and reddish plant down. It is a beautiful specimen of the nest of the species.

Pl. XXV. Fig. 1
TROCHILUS COLUBRIS
RUBY-THROATED HUMMINGBIRD.

Fig. 2.
POLIOPTILA CÆRULEA.
BLUE-GRAY GNATCATCHER.

PLATE XXVI.

SPIZELLA SOCIALIS—Chipping Sparrow
Spizella passerina—Chipping Sparrow
Illustrated by Virginia Jones

The nest was built in an apple tree. The foundation and superstructure are composed of fine rootlets, weed stems, fibers, and slender grasses. The lining of fine weed stems, cow hair, and long, black horsehairs. The eggs bear so little resemblance to any others of similar size, that even extremes can usually be identified at once. The identification of the nest, however, on account of the great variation in locality, position, and materials, is uncertain; still, one accustomed to the architecture of "the Chippy" will, generally, experience no difficulty in determining the species when the nest is met with.

What person, as a child, has not seen the tiny blue eggs, with their dark, irregular lines and spots, in the nest in the evergreen or grapevine beside the door, and watched with pleasure and wonder their transformation into scrawny, half-clothed little birds, that lift their heavy heads and open wide their mouths—which seem to be the greater part of them—when the parent-bird with some unlucky larva makes known her presence by fluttering wings and satisfied notes?

Pl. XXVI.
SPIZELLA SOCIALIS.
CHIPPING SPARROW.

PLATE XXVII.

ARDEA VIRESCENS—Green Heron (a.k.a. Fly-up-the-creek)

Butorides virescens—Green Heron

Illustrated by Virginia Jones

One of the most interesting sights I have ever seen in bird life was a Green Heron catching minnows. It had taken a position upon a small log, which was lying half immersed in a little stream. The current had washed a pocket under the log so that it formed a resort for chubs, silversides, and suckers. He was stretched out flat upon the log, with his neck drawn up, and bill resting close to the surface of the water. While I stood wondering at his queer position, he suddenly darted his head into the water and withdrew a minnow in his beak. This he swallowed and immediately renewed his position as before. I watched with admiration the skill and patience displayed by the little fisherman. Nearly every dip he brought up a fish, though obliged to wait ten to fifteen minutes in the concealed position before one would come within his reach. Every day this bird returned to his fishing place, until all the minnows in the pocket were either captured or became too wary for the tricks of their enemy.

The nest was taken from the limb of a wild cherry tree. It contained four fresh eggs. The structure, in comparison with some, is neat and small, but pretty fairly represents an average nest. This species often builds in colonies, like some of the other herons, but this is not always the case. In fact, it is a very common occurrence for a pair to make their summer home in some secluded little nook, apart from any of their near relatives.

PL XXVII.
ARDEA VIRESCENS.
GREEN HERON.

PLATE XXVIII.

PROGNE PURPUREA—Purple Martin

Progne subis—Purple Martin

Illustrated by Virginia Jones

Although the species is single brooded, like most other birds, they will lay a number of sets of eggs, if robbed. When the young are hatched, the parents become exceedingly noisy. Long before day and often during the night, the males attempt what they seem to consider a song. This consists of a series of noises resembling somewhat those produced by saw-filing, gritting the teeth, an ungreased wagon wheel, and the like.

The Martin is a watchful and pugnacious bird, and on this account his friendship is frequently cultivated, and his qualities utilized by giving him a home in the vicinity of the poultry yard, thereby assuring protection against the depredations of the hawk. He delights in maintaining his own rights, and often has combats with the bluebird, House Sparrow, and wren for the possession of a building site. I think the Purple Martin is usually victorious.

Plate XXVIII illustrates an old-fashioned Martin-box, with its female occupant. Boxes are generally made by people to represent houses, churches, or courthouses. These are often handsomely painted, and placed upon posts or house-tops; but I doubt if they are any more acceptable to the birds than the old-time gourd—with a hole cut in the side for an entrance, and a piece of branch driven in just beneath it for a perch—tied to a long pole set in the ground, or fastened in an upright position to a fence or gate-post.

*This is one of two illustrations in the book that includes the bird. The other is the Cliff Swallow, plate XLI.

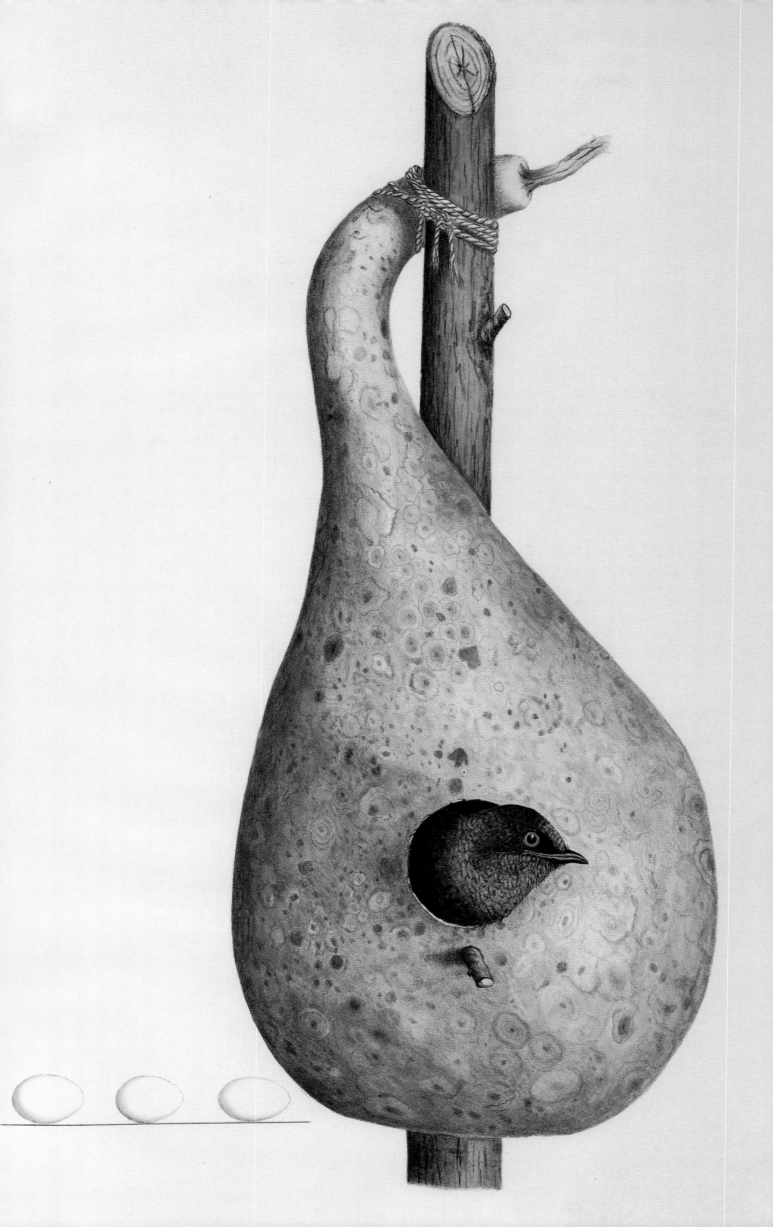

Pl. XXVIII.
PROGNE PURPUREA.
PURPLE MARTIN.

PLATE XXIX.

EUSPIZA AMERICANA—Black-throated Bunting

Spiza americana—Dickcissel

Illustrated by Virginia Jones

Of all our birds of the Fringillidae family, there is perhaps none much more interesting than the Black-throated Bunting. The male is clothed in a suit attractive and neat, is trim in form and his dress fits exceedingly well. The clover field is, above all others, his favorite. He delights to perch upon the top rail of a fence or upon a weed stalk and sing to his mate, who sits upon her treasures beneath the fragrant blossoms. When singing he seems unconscious of intruders unless his nest is approached too near. He then becomes silent and suddenly disappears, either to hide among the clover or to reappear at a place farther from the nest and again attract you with his song.

The nest was taken from a perpendicular fork of a stunted elm situated near a railroad track at the edge of a clover field. Four eggs constituted the complement. The middle egg is an average specimen in size, shape, and color.

From dawn until dusk he utters at short intervals, first from one post and then from another, but never far from his nest, those pleasantly monotonous notes, which, pronounced, sound like chip-chip-che-che; *and which, translated into English, may mean, as has been suggested: "Look! Look! See me here! See!"*

Pl. XXIX.
EUSPIZA AMERICANA
BLACK-THROATED BUNTING.

PLATE XXX.

MELOSPIZA MELODIA—Song Sparrow

Melospiza melodia—Song Sparrow

Illustrated by Virginia Jones

The nest and eggs were situated in a slight depression in a bank, sloping to a stream of water, and was protected only by the blades of bluegrass which surrounded it. The position is a characteristic one. The eggs in the nest are so in shadow that the average and extremes in size, color, and marking have been represented on a line beneath.

Pl. XXX.
MELOSPIZA MELODIA.
SONG SPARROW.

PLATE XXXI.

HARPORHYNCHUS RUFUS—Brown Thrush

Toxostoma rufum—Brown Thrasher

Illustrated by Virginia Jones

If driven from her nest, the female utters a peculiar alarm note, which at once summons her mate, who proves to be as big a scold as she is. If the nest contains young instead of eggs, both birds become exceedingly troubled, and solicitous for their safety; and exhibit in the highest degree, feeling sympathy and love for their offspring.

The nest illustrated was built in the fork of a haw tree, at the edge of a thick woods. The materials of construction consist of sticks, weed stems, old leaves, and rootlets. The external diameter of the structure is, on account of the position, a little less perhaps than usual. The middle egg is an average specimen.

Pl. XXXI.
HARPORHYNCHUS RUFUS.
BROWN THRUSH.

PLATE XXXII.

HELMINTHROPHAGA PINUS—Blue-winged Yellow Warbler

Vermivora cyanoptera—Blue-winged Warbler

Illustrated by Virginia Jones

Walking leisurely through the border of a woods, with a thick undergrowth of hazel, blackberry, and wild-rose bushes, I stopped to look about and to listen to the various bird songs, when, nearly at my feet, a little bird flew out, and was in an instant lost in the thick foliage. After a few moments search the nest was revealed, containing two eggs. Not being certain as to the identity of the species, I returned the following day and found the bird upon the nest. I had approached within a few yards of the spot and was cautiously peering to get a good look, when she disappeared among the neighboring bushes and began uttering a lisping chirp. These often repeated notes soon brought her mate, who uttered the same cry and seemed much disturbed. Both birds remained near their home during my stay, flying from one bush to another, but more frequently heard than seen.

This proved to be the nest and eggs of the Blue-winged Yellow Warbler, and is the one illustrated. It is built between a young elm and several blackberry stems. Its foundation is made principally of oak leaves, and rests upon the dead leaves which are lodged about the roots of the bushes. The superstructure and lining are composed entirely of grapevine bark. There is not much known in regard to the breeding habits of this species. This is more owing to the difficulty of finding the nest, however, than to the scarcity of the birds.

It is indeed wonderful that such tiny birds can manage such rough and crude materials as well as they do.

Pl. XXXII.
HELMINTHOPHAGA PINUS.
BLUE-WINGED YELLOW WARBLER.

PLATE XXXIII.

PYRANGA RUBRA (LINNAEUS) VIEILL—Scarlet Tanager

Piranga olivacea—Scarlet Tanager

Illustrated by Virginia Jones

I noticed one day, as I was driving, a nest which seemed to be a Scarlet Tanager, on an elm limb that projected across the road. With some difficulty, I drove the bird from her eggs by throwing clods at the limb. She perched upon a neighboring branch and began to peer about, stretching her slender neck to its utmost limit. The male was not seen, but I was told by a gentleman that he had just seen a tanager feeding in a hedge about half a mile away. This, I suppose, was her mate.

The nest was taken from the branch of an elm tree which overhung a country road. It is composed entirely of soft vine stems, except the lining, which is made of very clean, fine rootlets. The illustration gives a better idea of the arrangement of the materials of construction than can be conveyed by a description.

Pl. XXXIII.
PYRANGA RUBRA (Linn.) Vieill.
SCARLET TANAGER.

PLATE XXXIV.

PYRANGA AESTIVA—Summer Redbird

Piranga aestiva—Summer Tanager

Illustrated by Virginia Jones

The nest of the Summer Redbird is hard to find, even when the tree in which it is placed has been located. If there is a Summer Redbird in the woods in which you are, he is pretty sure to see you before you do him, and will at once give the alarm note to his mate, and endeavor to scold you from the premises. Excepting the Yellow-breasted Chat, he is the greatest scold in the woods. His voice is not harsh and loud, on the contrary, it is low and mellow, but there is in it a plaintiveness which expresses, plainer than words could do, the irritation of the bird, and his hearty wish that the intruder was out of his way. The female sits so closely upon her nest that the hand can almost be placed upon her before she will fly. When driven from her eggs she usually flies away silently, and hides among the foliage, but if she has young she will defend them bravely. She utters the same cry as the male when disturbed.

The nest was found in a hickory tree in the woods, with the center egg being the most typical one.

Pl. XXXIV.
PYRANGA ÆSTIVA.
SUMMER REDBIRD.

PLATE XXXV.

EMPIDONAX TRAILLII—Traill's Flycatcher

Empidonax traillii—Willow Flycatcher

Illustrated by Virginia Jones

From Dr. John Maynard Wheaton's State Report: "No bird is more wary when its nest is approached, quitting it as soon as an intruder comes within a dozen yards. I have seldom been able to discover the female on her nest, but, when disturbed, she retires to a safe distance, and utters a plaintive whit, expressive of her anxiety. During the breeding season the ordinary notes undergo some change, becoming a louder, deeper, hoyt-te-ar."*

The nest was taken from an elder bush, in a low piece of land beside a canal. It is in size, shape, materials, and position about an average specimen, save the bit of newspaper.

*All text quoted by Howard Jones in *Illustrations of the Nests and Eggs of Birds of Ohio* were incompletely cited, as standard conventions for citations did not exist at the time. Please see the copyright page for source citations.

Pl. XXXV.
EMPIDONAX TRAILLII.
TRAILL'S FLYCATCHER.

PLATE XXXVI.

CYANURUS CRISTATUS—Blue Jay
Cyanocitta cristata—Blue Jay
Illustrated by Virginia Jones

The blue and white plumage of the Blue Jay, together with his fine proportions, makes him one of the most conspicuous birds. His character I can perhaps best portray by comparing him to his near relative, the common crow, for in his method of thought and action he is very crowlike. In the summer he makes his living by robbing the nests of others, and none of the small forest birds know him but to fear him. He is always active, hopping about from branch to branch, and peering into every cluster of leaves, with his keen and cunning eye, in search of some home to destroy. The eggs of the Dove and Yellow-billed Cuckoo are not too large for him, and I am inclined to believe he would peck into common hen's eggs, if the opportunity afforded. A small egg he will carry from the nest to some safe place, and there suck the contents. Although an arrant coward when plundering a nest, and afraid of the smallest bird, he assumes great courage, and generally leads the rag-tag and bob-tail militia in their daytime attacks upon the Great Horned Owl. And it has frequently occurred to me, from the twinkle in his eye, that he is fully conscious that he is making a fine reputation for valor, where there is not the slightest danger. He will steal every thing he wants to eat, and any thing he wants and cannot eat, he will carry off and hide. But to counterbalance this natural depravity, he is a pretty fair songster, his notes being low and sweet, and in great contrast to his common catcalls.

The nest illustrated was taken from a pine-tree in a country lawn. The thorny sticks in the foundation were selected from the trimmings of a neighboring hedge. The eggs figured were selected from a large number, and the middle egg is the commonest pattern.

Notwithstanding the general meanness of the Jay Bird, some good things may be said of him.

PI XXXVI.
CYANURUS CRISTATUS.
BLUE JAY.

PLATE XXXVII.

PIPILO ERYTHROPHTHALMUS—Chewink (a.k.a. Ground Robin, Towhee)

Pipilo erythrophthalmus—Eastern Towhee

Illustrated by Virginia Jones

The male Chewink is much more frequently seen than the female, partly because he is a noisy fellow and of conspicuous plumage, but mainly, I think, because his partner is much more retiring in disposition. He is a clever cheat, and wherever he happens to be found during the nesting season, he behaves as if his home was within a few yards, when, in fact, it is rare to discover him within considerable distance of his nest.

The nest is very difficult to find on account of its resemblance to its surroundings. The nests that I have collected I have usually found by walking up to the female, and, until she would give the alarm note, the male would keep quiet and out of sight. Indeed, he seems to avoid going too near the nest, unless the female calls him. Both parents show great anxiety and solicitude for their nest and eggs, and especially for their young. The young run about some days before they can fly, and follow their mother wherever she calls. They are very active little chicks and slip along through the grass and brush rapidly.

The nest, which contained four eggs, was taken from an upland woods, dense with underbrush. It was situated in a bank of dead leaves, which had shifted and lodged against a small lichen-covered branch, part of a dead limb that the winds had blown from a tree near by.

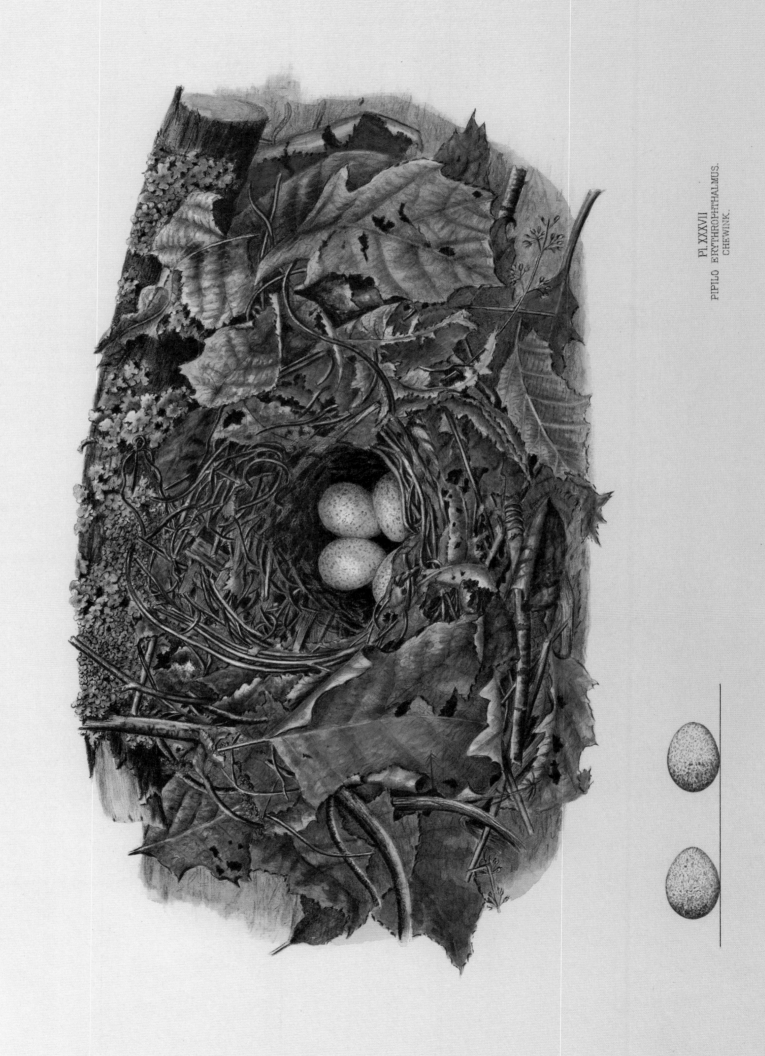

PLATE XXXVIII.

STURNELLA MAGNA—Meadow Lark

Sturnella magna—Eastern Meadowlark

Illustrated by Virginia Jones

The Meadow Lark is a very shy bird at all times, and particularly during the nesting season. They will rarely go near their nest when conscious they are observed, and they are always on the watch for danger. The female sits closely, and will not leave her home unless she is in imminent peril. When driven from her nest she often feigns lameness in leg and wing, and will flutter about, uttering a low cry in imitation of that of the young in distress, hoping in this way to divert the attention of the intruder, by tempting him to catch a wounded bird.

Larks are partial to country roads, and, at all seasons, are frequently seen perched upon the fence or feeding in the roadside grass. During the time the female is sitting, the male generally keeps guard from some neighboring bush or fence, occasionally singing a medley or uttering a few cheering notes. If approached he betrays anxiety by an uneasy jerk of his tail, and when he considers the danger past, sometimes he will fly directly to his mate upon the nest, perhaps to tell some trumped up story of his courage.

The nest, with four eggs, is a good specimen of the domed variety. It was lifted from its position in a clump of grass and placed upon the ground nearby, so that the drawing would show its composition and construction to better advantage. Below, two eggs are figured, representing the usual sizes and markings, as those in the nest are somewhat foreshortened and obscured.

PL. XXXVIII.
STURNELLA MAGNA.
MEADOW LARK.

PLATE XXXIX.

Fig. 1. PANDION HALIAETUS CAROLINENSIS—Fish Hawk (a.k.a. American Osprey)
Pandion haliaetus—Osprey
Illustrated by Howard Jones

I have frequently seen the Osprey, singly and in pairs, fishing in the rivers for suckers. From a great height the bird would plunge into water not more than three feet deep. Each time the Osprey descended like an arrow, struck the water with a sharp thud, and disappeared for several seconds. The last time I thought him hurt, as he extended his wings on the surface and remained motionless for a moment, then, with great effort, he arose from the water and in his talons carried, head foremost, a sucker over a foot long.

The center egg is probably the commonest size, shape, and pattern of marks.

Fig. 2. MELEAGRIS GALLOPAVO AMERICANA—Wild Turkey
Meleagris gallopavo—Wild Turkey
Illustrated by Howard Jones
Original text by Nelson Jones

The Wild Turkey is by far the most valuable and interesting of the birds indigenous to this continent. It surpasses all others in size and in beauty. Like most animals, it has quite strong attachments to place.

When the female builds her nest, she exercises wonderful care and precaution to keep the secret from the males and predators. She approaches the place with apparent indifference, but always by a circuitous route, differing with each visit, and when quitting the nest covers the eggs with old leaves and other light material common to the locality. The nest shows but little art and occupies in construction but little time.

Fig. 3. CATHARTES AURA—Turkey Buzzard
Carthartes aura—Turkey Vulture
Illustrated by Howard Jones

Whenever one Turkey Buzzard is seen, close inspection will generally discern more, for they are gregarious at all seasons. When carrion is found by one, others soon come, until a large flock is assembled. When upon the ground they move about awkwardly, making a striking contrast with their grace of motion during flight. When they start to fly, they leap into the air with a clumsy jump, flap their wings rapidly until they are some feet above the surface, and then begin to sail in increasing circles.

The center egg is the commonest form.

*While the Jones family had initially intended to depict the nests of the 130 birds mentioned in the prospectus, it became apparent that some nests were too large to collect or could not be found at all, in which cases only the eggs of these species were illustrated.

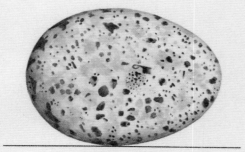  

Pl. XXXIX Fig.1.
PANDION HALIAETUS CAROLINENSIS.
FISH HAWK.

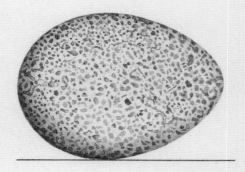 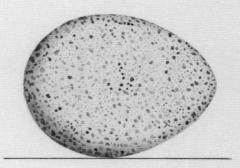 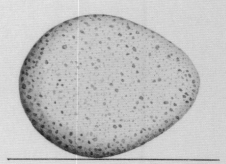

Fig. 2.
MELEAGRIS GALLOPAVO AMERICANA.
WILD TURKEY.

Fig. 3.
CATHARTES AURA.
TURKEY BUZZARD.

PLATE XL.

ICTERUS SPURIUS—Orchard Oriole

Icterus spurius—Orchard Oriole

Illustrated by Virginia Jones

The Orchard Oriole is a beautiful and graceful bird, and the male is a fine songster. Several pairs of them usually build quite close together, sometimes two nests being in the same tree. During the mating and nesting season, the males fly about rapidly from tree to tree and from branch to branch, repeating at every stop, and sometimes during flight, the pleasant notes of their song. In early morning their voices can be heard above the rest of the feathered tribe with which they associate, few, if any, birds of equal size being able to compete with them in roundness and loudness of tone. When the young are hatched both parents show great concern for their safety.

One of the prettiest objects I have ever seen in bird-life was a home containing five young Orioles. I decided to take two of them, and as the remaining ones would not stay in the nest, having jumped from it, I brought it along with me and hung it up in my room. At night they would cuddle into this feather-lined basket and sleep quietly until dawn. The little orphans soon became very tame, and grew rapidly on pounded beef and hard-boiled egg. My sister, Genevieve, now took charge of them, placing them in a large cage with a number of other birds. Here they became so gentle and happy that they would fly upon her finger at the door of the cage.

The nest was taken from an apple tree. It was situated at the extreme of a limb eight feet from the ground.

Pl. XL.
ICTERUS SPURIUS.
ORCHARD ORIOLE.

PLATE XLI.

PETROCHELIDON LUNIFRONS—Cliff Swallow

Petrochelidon pyrrhonota—Cliff Swallow

Illustrated by Virginia Jones

Before civilization afforded suitable nesting places, the species built against rocky cliffs. Until the present century these birds were scarce, and while distributed throughout the United States, their colonies were only met with here and there at great distances. But civilization having decreased their enemies and increased suitable building sites, they have greatly multiplied.

With no apparent cause, a colony will desert a locality where they have built for years, never to return. On the other hand, when they have taken possession of a site, no amount of annoyance can persuade them to abandon it. When disturbed they show great uneasiness, flying in circles about the intruder and snapping their bills in angry manner. The winter season loosens their nests, and they fall to the ground.

The nest was ten feet from the ground, the entrance facing the side of a barn. It was selected from dozens of nests from different colonies, as a typical specimen in size and shape. The female is represented peering from the entrance, just before flying away. The middle egg has the most common form.

Pl. XLI.
PETROCHELIDON LUNIFRONS.
CLIFF SWALLOW.

PLATE XLII.

THRYOMANES BEWICKI—Bewick's Wren

Thryomanes bewickii—Bewick's Wren

Illustrated by Virginia Jones

This species was discovered and named in the year 1821 by Mr. Audubon, but nothing was known of its breeding habits until 1844. According to *North American Birds*, Mr. Spencer Fullerton Baird, an ornithologist, in this year, discovered its nest and eggs.

The nest and eggs were taken from a barn.

PLATE XLIII.

ASTRAGALINUS TRISTIS—American Goldfinch (a.k.a. Lettuce Bird, Thistle Bird, Yellowbird)

Spinus tristis—American Goldfinch

Illustrated by Virginia Jones

As soon as the quarrels of mating are over and the nest is seriously thought of, each pair attends strictly to family duties, being greatly attached to their home and young. If their nest is robbed or destroyed another is generally built, and, sometimes, even a third is constructed, but, unless molested, only one set is laid by each pair during a single season.

The song of the American Goldfinch is not remarkable for anything but constancy. The prominent notes are the same, at all times and all places. The sunniest day of May puts no more expression into them than the bleakest day of December. On this account, these birds have endeared themselves to me, as their song is always happy and cheerful. Especially does it seem welcome and suggestive of wild flowers and balmy breezes, even when the barren trees and frozen ground have hushed all voices but the melancholy whistle of the Cherrybird, the croak of the Nuthatch, or the cold and shivering chirp of the Sparrow.

The nest was taken from a large thistle, beside a branch from a spring, near a public road. It was about four feet from the ground. It contained five eggs. The eggs figured were selected from several nests. Externally, it is covered with catkins, and within, it is compactly lined with a thick layer of thistle down. The center one has the most common pattern.

Pl. XLIII.
ASTRAGALINUS TRISTIS.
AMERICAN GOLDFINCH.

PLATE XLIV.

MELANERPES ERYTHROCEPHALUS—Red-headed Woodpecker

Melanerpes erythrocephalus—Red-headed Woodpecker

Illustrated by Virginia Jones

The presence of the Red-headed Woodpecker, being conspicuous by his national colors and very quarrelsome and noisy, is generally known wherever he is.

After days have been spent constructing a home, a Bluebird or House Wren may decide to possess it, and such an unceasing war is waged against the owners that they will abandon it, rather than be in a continual fight. Sometimes a pair of Red-heads, instead of building, will select an old house of some other woodpecker, or even a natural cavity.

The young are homely little things, and, when fully fledged, are so cowardly that they will frequently remain in the nest, calling for food, when they are abundantly able to care for themselves. The parents are, however, exceedingly indulgent, and seem strongly attached to their offspring, feeding and protecting them even long after quitting the nest. Yet, notwithstanding this solicitude for their progeny, they frequently starve to death all of the brood but one or two. In every brood there is one bird older and stronger than the rest. Being stronger at the start than his brothers and sisters, and, each day getting more food, he gains more strength; and, gaining more strength, he gets each day more food. While this double-acting system progresses, the reverse is happening to his mates, until, in extreme cases, they actually die of starvation, and are not even carried out of the nest by the parents.

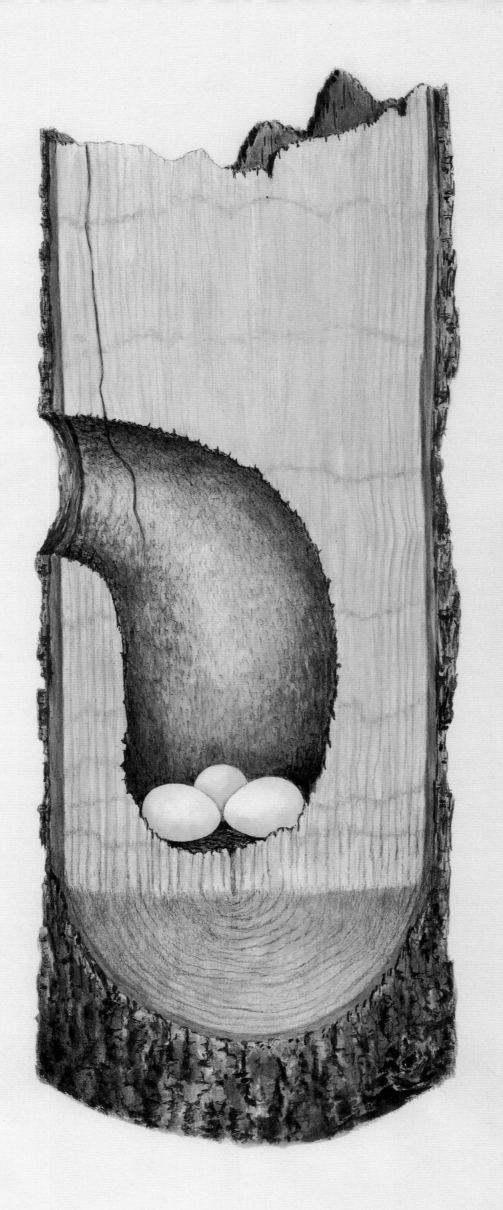

PL. XLIV.
MELANERPES ERYTHROCEPHALUS.
RED-HEADED WOODPECKER.

PLATE XLV.

Fig. 1. TRINGOIDES MACULARIUS—Spotted Sandpiper
Actitis macularius—Spotted Sandpiper
Illustrated by Howard Jones

The eggs seem out of all proportion to the size of the bird. It is really wonderful how such a little body can safely lay them. The young run about as soon as hatched, and follow their parents wherever they lead. They are neat and dainty, and, when walking, tilt themselves in a characteristic manner, which has given them the vulgar name of "teeter-tails." The eggs are colored from blown specimens about a year old. The colors do not fade much, but with time they lose the brilliancy they possessed when the eggs were fresh.

Fig. 2. OXYECHUS VOCIFERUS—Killdeer
Charadrius vociferus—Killdeer
Illustrated by Howard Jones

The Killdeer is a tame and unsuspicious bird, except during the breeding season. At this time they are extremely solicitous. It is easy to tell when a pair have a nest of young by their circling flight and pleading cries, but it is very difficult to locate the nest by their actions, as they are purposely misleading.

The middle egg depicts the most common pattern.

Fig. 3. ASIO ACCIPITRINUS—Short-eared Owl
Asio flammeus—Short-eared Owl
Illustrated by Howard Jones

The food of these owls consists principally of mice, and consequently they frequent the grassy marshlands in which the field mice delight.

The center egg shows perhaps the most frequently observed pattern.

Fig. 4. CORVUS FRUGIVORUS—Common Crow
Corvus brachyrhynchos—American Crow
Illustrated by Howard Jones

The Common Crow, except in cases of partial or complete albinism, is so intensely and uniformly black that the name has become a synonym for the color. In intelligence, the crow is surpassed by none of our native birds, and equaled by few. It is possessed of a mind rapid in action, deep in penetration, and logical in method. All of these qualities, together with the fact that the moral code of the Crow does not exist, make it a bird feared by the feathery tribe and despised by man. By nature, the Crow is a thief, and hungry young at home increase their prowess and bravery.

The middle egg depicts the most common pattern.

Pl.XLV. Fig.1.
TRINGOIDES MACULARIUS.
SPOTTED SANDPIPER.

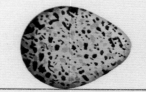
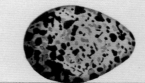

Fig.2.
OXYECHUS VOCIFERUS.
KILLDEER.

Fig.3.
ASIO ACCIPITRINUS.
SHORT-EARED OWL.

Fig.4.
CORVUS FRUGIVORUS.
COMMON CROW.

PLATE XLVI.

TELMATODYTES PALUSTRIS—Long-billed Marsh Wren

Cistothorus palustris—Marsh Wren

Illustrated by Virginia Jones

Long-billed Marsh Wrens seem to have sentinels all about their breeding grounds whose duty it is to give the alarm (a squeaky little note), on the approach of danger. Once the alarm is sounded, it is carried from one to another, until every bird is aroused. This habit makes it very difficult to catch the birds in, or even near, their nests.

Every ornithologist has noted the fact that but few nests of the whole number found contain eggs, and many guesses have been made to account for the construction of so many useless houses. The center egg depicts the most common pattern.

Pl. XLVI.
TELMATODYTES PALUSTRIS.
LONG-BILLED MARSH WREN.

PLATE XLVII.

Fig. 1. HYDROCHELIDON LARIFORMIS SURINAMENSIS—Black Tern
Chlidonias niger—Black Tern

Illustrated by Howard Jones

The flight of the Black Tern is graceful and even careless. It sails through the air with the ease consequent upon a large expanse of wing and a small, light body. Now circling up, now dropping like a feather upon some log lodged in the current. Here it sits, apparently contemplating suicide, then suddenly, as though some uncontrollable circumstance had decided the matter, it starts off to search for food.

Fig. 2. CERYLE ALCYON—Belted Kingfisher
Megaceryle alcyon—Belted Kingfisher

Illustrated by Howard Jones

The Kingfisher is a bird of striking outline, beautiful plumage, and very interesting habits. In the vicinity of its nest, it is quiet and rarely seen. The female becomes greatly attached to the locality of her first nest, and will build year after year in the same bank, either deepening and cleaning out the old excavation or making a new one nearby. The young are helpless things, and require a deal of patient care and hard work to rear and teach the skill of proficient fishermen. To dive into the water and catch a minnow is no easy task, and much practice is necessary before they are able to support themselves.

Fig. 3. GALLINULA GALEATA—Florida Gallinule
Porphyrio martinica—Purple Gallinule

Illustrated by Howard Jones

The Florida Gallinule is in many respects a curious bird. The middle egg shows perhaps the most common form.

Fig. 4. FULICA AMERICANA—American Coot
Fulica americana—American Coot

Illustrated by Howard Jones

"They are shy, but rarely take wing, preferring to swim than to fly to a safe retreat. Sometimes they may be forced to fly; in this event, they rise awkwardly from the water, skim over its surface, and alight a few hundred yards away." —Dr. F. W. Langdon, *Journal of the Cincinnati Society of Natural History*

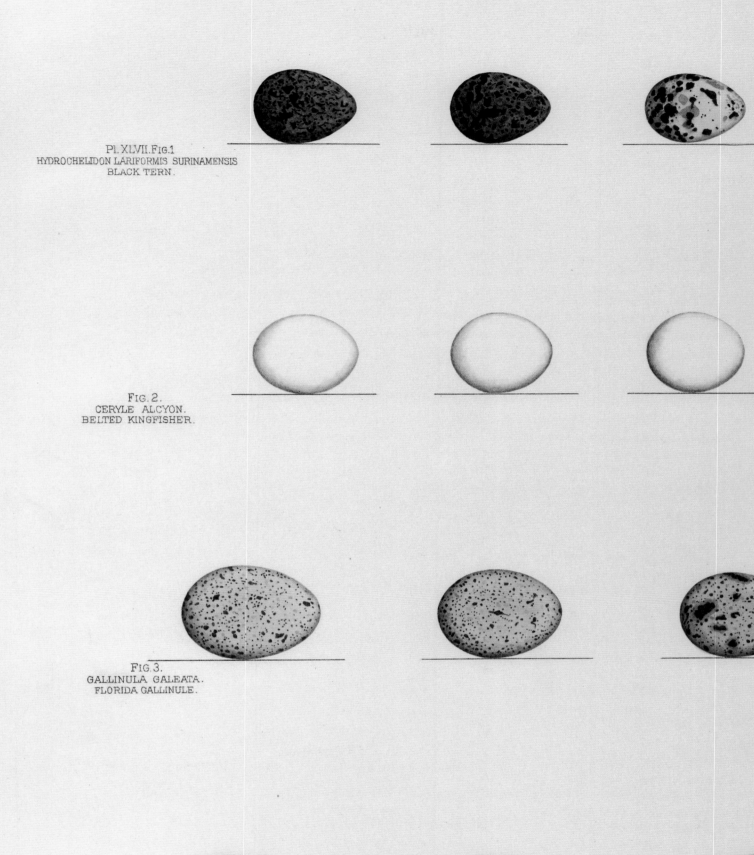

Pl. XLVII. Fig. 1
HYDROCHELIDON LARIFORMIS SURINAMENSIS
BLACK TERN.

Fig. 2.
CERYLE ALCYON.
BELTED KINGFISHER.

Fig. 3.
GALLINULA GALEATA.
FLORIDA GALLINULE.

Fig. 4
FULICA AMERICANA.
AMERICAN COOT.

PLATE XLVIII.

Fig. 1. VIREO NOVEBORACENSIS—White-eyed Vireo
Vireo griseus—White-eyed Vireo
Illustrated by Virginia Jones

"The White-eyed Vireo has always been notable, even in groups of birds whose spirit is high, for its irritable temperament; and, during the breeding season, nothing can surpass the petulance and irascibility which it displays when its home is too nearly approached, and the fuss it makes when its temper is ruffled in this way. It skips about in a panicky state, as regardless of exposure as a virago haranguing the crowd on a street corner, seemingly at such loss for adequate expletives that we may fancy it quite ready to say 'Thank you,' if somebody would only swear a little.... Their uneasiness is chiefly exhibited during the breeding season, and all their vehemence is but the excess of their concern for their little families…their ardor exhausts itself when the occasion is past, and, what had been excessive solicitude gives way to simple sprightliness and vivacity." —Dr. Elliott Coues, *Birds of the Colorado Valley*

Fig. 2. POOECETES GRAMINEUS—Grass Finch (a.k.a. Bay-winged Bunting)
Pooecetes gramineus—Vesper Sparrow
Illustrated by Virginia Jones

The nest is a very simple affair. The foundation and superstructure consist chiefly of a few weed stems, grasses, straws, and rootlets, entwined and matted together, and the lining is made of a few grasses, rootlets, and horsehairs. The song of this species is pleasing and is most frequently heard in the evening, often after other birds are silent.

Pl. XLVIII. Fig. 1.
VIREO NOVEBORACENSIS.
WHITE-EYED VIREO.

Fig 2.
POŒCETES GRAMINEUS
GRASS FINCH.

PLATE XLIX.

Fig. 1. TINNUNCULUS SPARVERIUS—Sparrow Hawk

Falco sparverius—American Kestrel

Illustrated by Howard Jones

During the first bright days of spring the Sparrow Hawks choose their nesting-place; and, although cold may delay egg-laying some weeks, the pair remain in the neighborhood of their home, going in and out at frequent intervals, as if the contemplation of the future responsibilities was a source of the greatest pleasure. The middle egg is the usual pattern.

Fig. 2. ACCIPITER COOPERI—Cooper's Hawk

Accipiter cooperii—Cooper's Hawk

Illustrated by Howard Jones

I raised from a nestling a male Cooper's Hawk, and kept him until nearly a year. He was an interesting pet, full of cunning and boldness. He became so tame that he had the liberty of the town. He would wander about from tree to house-top, and would sometimes be gone a whole day. He was very fond of buggy riding, and would sit on the dashboard for hours, manifesting the greatest interest in the objects passed.

Fig. 3. BUTEO LINEATUS—Red-shouldered Hawk

Buteo lineatus—Red-shouldered Hawk

Illustrated by Howard Jones

A wet season affects the material appearance of the eggs, as the coloring matter of the markings is quite soluble in water. If showers occur, the eggs exposed will be more dingy, cloudy, and nest-stained than if dry weather prevails.

The pairs remain mated throughout the year. A pair will occupy the same nest for a number of years, if undisturbed, adding the necessary repairs each spring. The Red-tailed Hawk has the same habit of remodeling its old nest, year after year, instead of building an entirely new structure.

Fig. 4. BUTEO BOREALIS—Red-tailed Hawk (a.k.a. Hen Hawk)

Buteo jamaicensis—Red-tailed Hawk

Illustrated by Howard Jones

The Red-tailed Hawk has many enemies. But not withstanding, the species is plentiful. This hawk, like all of the family, is very intelligent, and is expert in avoiding danger.

During the period of egg laying and incubation, the male is watchful and shows his mate much attention. He often brings food to her, and, when the young are hatched, he becomes solicitous for their welfare and hunts the greater part of the day for their support.

Pl. XLIX. FIG. 1.
TINNUNCULUS SPARVERIUS
SPARROW HAWK.

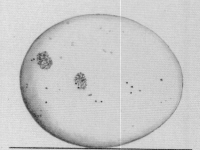

FIG. 2.
ACCIPITER COOPERI.
COOPERS HAWK.

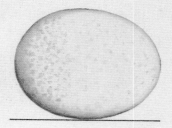

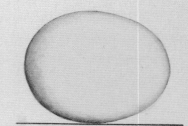

FIG. 3.
BUTEO LINEATUS.
RED-SHOULDERED HAWK.

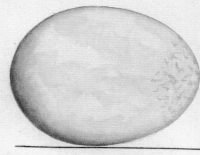

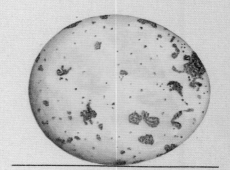

FIG. 4.
BUTEO BOREALIS.
RED-TAILED HAWK.

PLATE L.

TROGLODYTES AEDON—House Wren

Troglodytes aedon—House Wren

Illustrated by Virginia Jones

The House Wren frequents outhouses and dwellings in town and country, and may place its nest in any sheltered cranny. It is fond of human society, and quite generally takes advantage of the protection which the works and presence of man afford. Curious and unexpected situations are sometimes chosen for the nest: a buggy top, a bee hive, an old boot or hat, or the sleeve or pocket of a coat—in fact, none of the hundreds of places that the rubbish about a house offers can escape the inquisitive search of this delightful little bird when on the lookout for a building site.

Pl. L.
TROGLODYTES AEDON.
HOUSE WREN.

PLATE LI.

SETOPHAGA RUTICILLA—American Redstart

Setophaga ruticilla—American Redstart

Illustrated by Virginia Jones

The nest was found in dense upland woods, situated twelve feet from the ground on a slightly inclined hickory sapling. It is constructed so that the twig runs through it, between the lining and the superstructure. Its foundation and superstructure are composed of flaxen fibers, long shreds of the inner bark of grapevine, and balls and strings of snow-white web from a peculiar plant louse, which infested the maples the past year. The grapevine bark is most abundant around the rim. The lining is composed of very finely split grasses, long black horsehairs, and one black feather. But whatever the materials or external dimensions, the diameter of the cavity is very uniform.

The middle eggs show perhaps the most common form.

Pl. LI.
SETOPHAGA RUTICILLA.
AMERICAN REDSTART.

PLATE LII.

AMPELIS CEDRORUM—Cedar Wax-wing (a.k.a. Cedar Bird, Cherry Bird)

Bombycilla cedrorum—Cedar Waxwing

Illustrated by Virginia Jones

The Cedar Wax-wing is of beautiful form and feather, and is especially attractive on account of its handsome crest and "wax-tipped" secondaries (short, blunt flight feathers along the inner edge of the wing, close to the body). The vermilion wax-like tips are most plentiful on old birds, and, in very fine specimens, are not limited to the secondaries, but may be found also on the tail feathers. The Cedar Bird is said to have a very low song; ordinarily, it utters but a single note, a squeaking whistle of high pitch and peculiar timber. Its domestic life is largely a pantomime show. The billing and cooing is carried on with but an occasional word, and the young are apparently deaf and dumb. Their intelligence is of low order. They are great gormandizers—fearless when hungry, and stupid when satiated.

The nest illustrated was taken from a small elm tree. It is composed principally of split weed stems, fine rootlets, dead leaves of the elm, strings, and a bunch of linen ravelings. The lining differs from the foundation and superstructure only in being made of the best quality of the materials. The coarsest weed-stems and rootlets are exterior, the finest within. The center egg is perhaps nearest the average in all respects.

PLATE LIII.

Fig. 1. MELOSPIZA PALUSTRIS—Swamp Sparrow
Melospiza georgiana—Swamp Sparrow
Illustrated by Virginia Jones

The Swamp Sparrow has no song except during the nesting season. At this time it has an animated melody which it frequently utters from the top of some low bush, very much after the manner of the Song Sparrow, but its notes are by no means so attractive.

In the illustration the nest is shown turned over on its side, showing its size, shape, and structure. It is made principally of coarse grasses and frayed weed stems, a few rootlets are to be seen in the foundation, and the lining is composed of grasses. When in position, the rim of the nest was on a level with the surrounding sod, and a long tuft of grass concealed it from above, and protected it from the weather.

Fig. 2. CHAETURA PELASGICA—Chimney Swift (a.k.a. Chimney Swallow)
Chaetura pelagica—Chimney Swift
Illustrated by Virginia Jones

The Chimney Swift, in many of its habits, is very peculiar, and its nest is certainly a curious and ingenious piece of workmanship. The material for the nest is obtained while flying, and in a remarkable manner. Having selected a site for their nest, the birds busy themselves gathering twigs every morning and evening until it is completed. Locust and fruit trees furnish the sticks for the majority of nests, as they generally have numerous dead branches. The Swift, having chosen a tree from which the material is to be obtained, circles about it until a suitable twig is espied, then flies at it in a gently curving or straight line, in such a direction that it can be seized in the bill and broken off by the momentum acquired by the flight. Both male and female gather sticks. It is probable, however, that the female does the greater part of the work. The nest illustrated was built in a hollow apple tree.

After the young are safely reared, the life of the Chimney Swift becomes a great holiday. All day they fly about in scattered communities, and at night collect in some favorite chimney to roost. If, with superhuman power, one could divine the thoughts and emotions, the pleasures and hardships of the lives within that long, dark, and often sooty tube that the Chimney Swallow calls home, what sensational bird-history it would make!

Pl.LIII.Fig.1.
MELOSPIZA PALUSTRIS.
SWAMP SPARROW.

Fig.2.
CHAETURA PELASGICA.
CHIMNEY SWIFT.

PLATE LIV.

Fig. 1. MYIARCHUS CRINITUS—Great Crested Flycatcher
Myiarchus crinitus—Great Crested Flycatcher
Illustrated by Howard Jones

The Great Crested Flycatchers are very quarrelsome and tyrannical among themselves, or at least they appear to be, as they are continually scolding and complaining to each other and engaging in fights. This, however, may all be in fun, and their notes, which are so harsh and grating to the human ear, that when once heard are never forgotten, may convey to each other very pleasant and peaceful ideas.

    The most constant substance of their nest is cast-off snakeskin. It is commonly placed about the rim in little pieces, but it sometimes occurs in large sheets and in wrinkled sections in various parts of the structure. As a rule, the nest is not very clean and tidy, and it may be that the snakeskin used in the nest has an odor pleasant to the birds.

Fig. 2. PASSER DOMESTICUS—English Sparrow
Passer domesticus—House Sparrow
Illustrated by Howard Jones

It is astonishing with what courage and vigor English Sparrows take possession of any available hole, crevice, or nook, and with what pluck and stubbornness they defend their assumed rights. Much has been written against this remarkable bird, as well as much in its favor. That it is of some value in destroying noxious insects can hardly be denied, but it is also true, I think, that it prefers other food. It seems to be peaceable enough with other birds, but quarrels some with its own species.

    The center egg depicts perhaps the most common size and pattern.

Fig. 3. MOLOTHRUS ATER—Cowbird
Molothrus ater—Brown-headed Cowbird
Illustrated by Howard Jones

The Cowbird does not build a nest, preferring to deposit her eggs in those of other birds. The Cowbird is a coward, and never takes forcible possession of a nest, but, finding one unprotected, she occupies it for a minute or two and then sneaks away, apparently satisfied that her young one will be well able to hold its own in company with the strangers. The fact that the maternal cares are by this species imposed upon others, and that the mother herself hastens to the mountains during the most heated time of the summer, suggests the probability of the Cowbird belonging to some ultrafashionable circle of society.

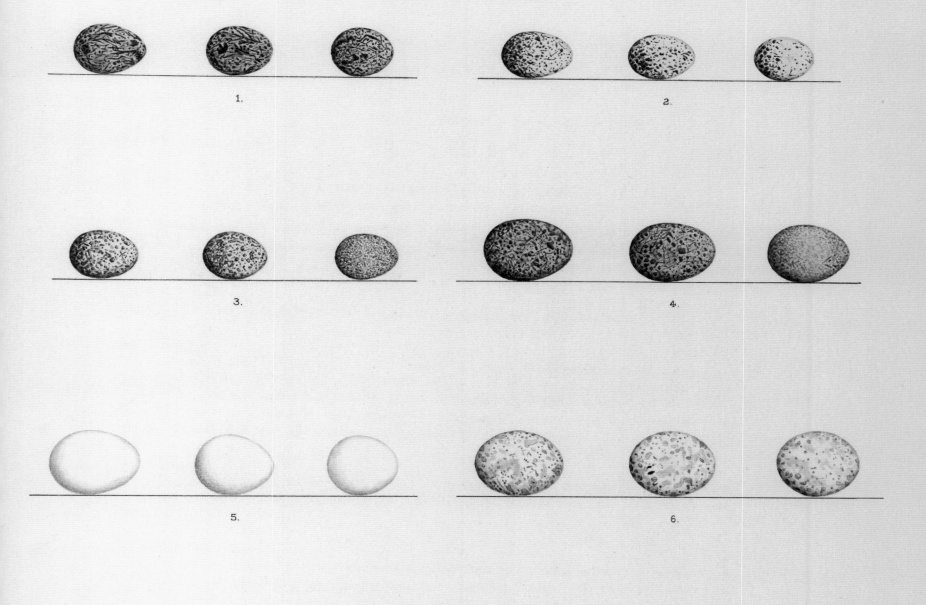

1.

2.

3.

4.

5.

6.

7.

Pl.LIV.

Fig.1. MYIARCHUS CRINITUS.
GREAT CRESTED FLYCATCHER.

Fig.2. PASSER DOMESTICUS.
ENGLISH SPARROW.

Fig.3. MOLOTHRUS ATER.
COWBIRD.

Fig.4 CHORDEILES POPETUE.
NIGHTHAWK.

Fig.5. COLAPTES AURATUS.
YELLOW-SHAFTED FLICKER.

Fig.6. CAPRIMULGUS VOCIFERUS.
WHIP-POOR-WILL

Fig.7. ARDEA HERODIAS.
GREAT BLUE HERON.

PLATE LIV.

Fig. 4. CHORDEILES POPETUE—Nighthawk
Chordeiles minor—Common Nighthawk
Illustrated by Howard Jones

The name "Nighthawk" is very improperly applied to the species under consideration. Undoubtedly it is most frequently seen between sundown and dark, and between dawn and sunrise, owing to the fact that the insects upon which it feeds are at these times upon the wing. But at all hours of the day this "Hawk" flies about. On the wing the Nighthawk is very active, but owing to the innumerable angles and curves inharmoniously joined, its flight is far from graceful, yet it is light and easy.

Wherever the "Hawks" abound, the eggs may be looked for in the most exposed and barren places—places which receive the sun's rays during the greater part of the day. The natural surroundings of the spot selected are seldom, if ever, disturbed; the eggs being laid in a slight depression, or among pebbles, which prevent their rolling. The Nighthawk is much attached to her eggs and young, and gives them the most watchful attention. The eggs are difficult to find even when at your feet, owing to their protective colors.

Fig. 5. COLAPTES AURATUS—Yellow-shafted Flicker
(a.k.a. Yellow Hammer, Flickup, Golden-winged Woodpecker, High-holer)
Colaptes auratus—Northern Flicker
Illustrated by Howard Jones

The Yellow-shafted Flicker frequents partially cleared land and fields, with here and there a decayed tree or tree trunk still standing, in preference to heavily wooded districts. Although shy, it is not afraid to venture into the orchard and lawn, and even at times into town. When the nesting season arrives, a dead limb or trunk is chosen for the site from among the trees in its accustomed haunts. Occasionally the nest is excavated in a gatepost, a telegraph pole, or some such place on the most frequented country thoroughfares.

When found upon her eggs, the Yellow-shafted Flicker hastens to escape, and once out of the hole, flies away to a safe distance. Occasionally a bird will show fight, but this is exceptional.

PLATE LIV.

Fig. 6. CAPRIMULGUS VOCIFERUS—Whip-poor-will
Caprimulgus vociferus—Eastern Whip-poor-will
Illustrated by Howard Jones

During the daytime the Whip-poor-will frequents the densest woods, preferably rocky ravines, where the sun rarely penetrates on account of the thick foliage of the trees and underbrush, and in such a locality it lays its eggs, placing them upon a shelving rock, or upon the ground among fallen leaves. Occasionally they are deposited beside a fallen log on the decayed wood chips, scattered by squirrels and Grouse, or occasionally upon a broad leaf spread flat upon the ground. No materials are carried for the nest, nor are the natural surroundings usually disturbed.

Usually only a single Whip-poor-will is seen at a time. In May and June they are much less numerous than in the fall. During the day they sit about on old logs, on the lower branches of trees, and upon the ground, in the most retired places, apparently sleeping. When flushed they utter no note, but fly off like a bat for a short distance and alight. If caution is used, one can approach very close. They seldom cry out during the day, unless it is exceptionally dark; but as soon as night comes on they repeat at short intervals their notes, which have by some lively imagination been likened to the words whip poor will. The sounds, however, bear no closer resemblance to these words than to many others.

Fig. 7. ARDEA HERODIAS—Great Blue Heron
Ardea herodias—Great Blue Heron
Illustrated by Howard Jones

The Great Blue Heron is a bird that commands attention and excites admiration, whether it be seen alive or dead. Its graceful form, beautiful plumage, and natural surroundings, all combine to make a harmony difficult to surpass. Besides, it is a bird of great judgment and much cunning, and is an expert in avoiding danger. Its food consists chiefly of fish, which it catches by wading out in the shallows of streams and along the shores of ponds. It will stand for hours in the water up to its knees, and every little while, swift as an arrow, it shoots out its long neck and dives its head under the water after an unfortunate fish, which it seizes in its bill and immediately swallows.

The flight of the Great Blue Heron is slow, but well sustained. Its wings are very large for the weight of its body, and consequently, comparatively few strokes are made in a minute. When wounded it will fight either man or dog, and may prove a dangerous antagonist.

As a rule, sets of eggs are much more uniform in color than this one.

PLATE LV.

CHONDESTES GRAMMICA—Lark Finch

Calamospiza melanocorys—Lark Bunting

Illustrated by Virginia Jones

Different from other sparrows, the Lark Finch runs instead of hops, and it is not uncommon to see a number running along the road like quail.

The illustrated nest and eggs, found situated on a hillside in a clover field, in a slight natural concavity near the footstalks of red clover, may be taken as a good example of the architecture of the Lark Finch. The nest is thickest about the rim and thinnest at the center of the bottom. At the center of the bottom of the nest, the middle layer is wanting, and as the external structure is at this point almost absent also, the lining rests nearly upon the ground. The materials of construction vary somewhat in different nests, according to the fancy of different birds for this or that material, and also according to its abundance.

Pl. LVI.
CHONDESTES GRAMMICA.
LARK FINCH.

PLATE LVI.

PICUS PUBESCENS—Downy Woodpecker

Picoides pubescens—Downy Woodpecker

Illustrated by Virginia Jones

As with other woodpeckers, the nest consists simply of an excavation in dead and generally semidecayed wood. Plate LVI represents a sectional view of a nest and eggs. It was in a willow stump about five feet from the ground. The Downy Woodpecker is a nervous, active bird, and is constantly occupied. During the time which the female is sitting, the male often excavates one or more small cavities in some neighboring tree, with no other object apparently than to be at work. He is very attentive to his partner all the while, and carries her choice morsels of food. When the young are hatched, he is equally solicitous with the mother, and the pair seldom go far from home. The plumage of the young is lemon-yellow where their parent's is white; this makes them even handsomer than when older, notwithstanding they have not the scarlet patch on their heads, so characteristic of all woodpeckers.

The young when two weeks old can fly, but they stay around the tree in which they were hatched for some time after, going in and out of their houses at will. At this age they are very pretty, fat, and saucy.

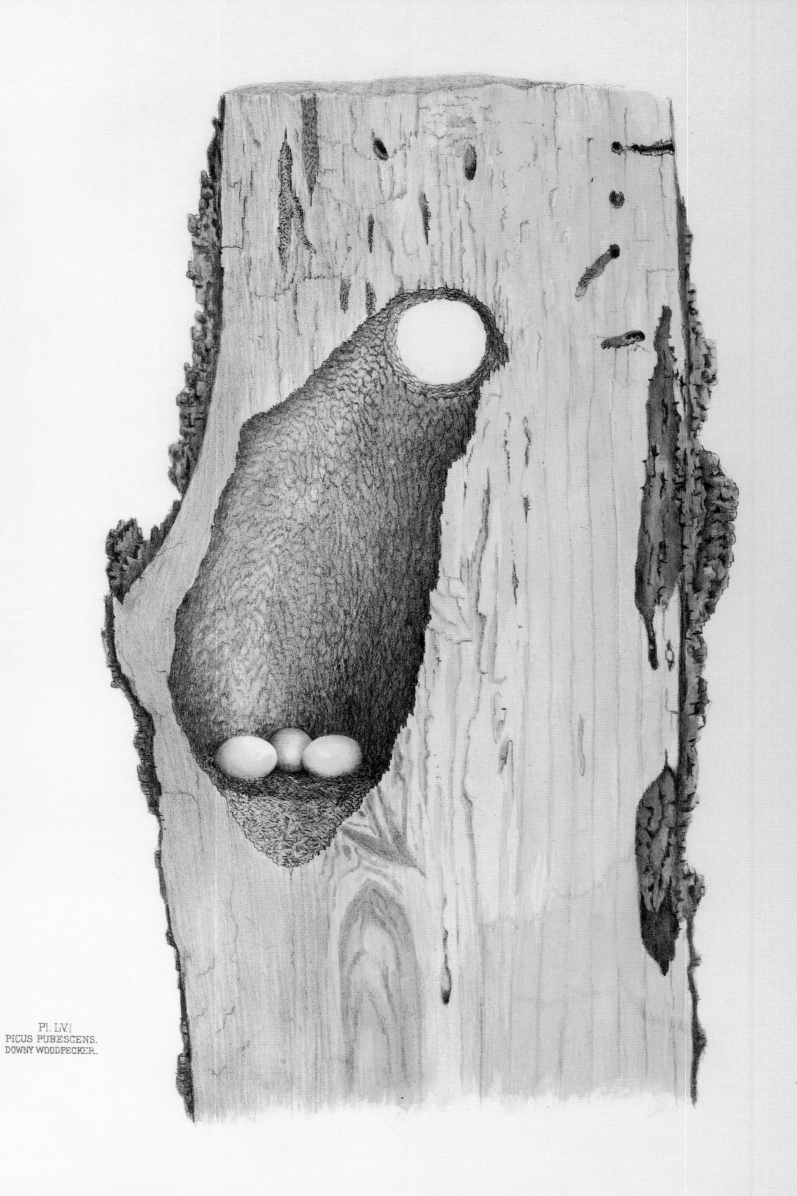

Pl. LVI.
PICUS PUBESCENS.
DOWNY WOODPECKER.

PLATE LVII.

DENDROECA PENNSYLVANICA—Chestnut-sided Warbler

Dendroica pensylvanica—Chestnut-sided Warbler

Illustrated by Virginia Jones

As a site for a nest, the Chestnut-sided Warbler generally selects a bush or low sapling in a thicket, about the border of the timberland where it makes its home; but occasionally a similar position is chosen in the interior of the woods. The coarser parts of the nest consist of several wide strips of the inner bark of some forest tree, and a number of blades of grass. They are arranged circularly, and are secured to the branches in some places by being wrapped several times, and in others they are bound down with web or silken threads from cocoons. The bark and grass form a loose foundation, upon and within which is placed the superstructure of gray fibers and light-brownish, wiry weed stems, and round tendrils from some climber. There is great uniformity in the size of these fibers, many of which have been split to reduce their thickness.

The nests and eggs illustrated were found in a hazel fork, in a dense thicket of briars and other bushes, within a few yards of a country road. It is a good example of the architecture of this species.

The materials are carried which are dexterously worked into one of the most beautiful and substantial specimens of woodland architecture.

Pl. LVII.
DENDRŒCA PENNSYLVANICA.
CHESTNUT-SIDED WARBLER.

PLATE LVIII.

HYLOCICHLA FUSCESCENS—Wilson's Thrush
Catharus fuscescens—Veery
Illustrated by Virginia Jones

All writers agree that this Thrush is a timid bird and so shy as to avoid more than a glance from its biographer. Even while sitting the female shows little of that anxiety and fearlessness of danger which the Robin, for instance, exhibits when her home is being inspected.

The nest illustrated was in a damp, shady ravine and contained four eggs. The nest of this species, like that of the Wood Thrush, is built in retired woods, where the ground is damp and the trees are mossy, and in shady ravines beside running springs and boggy earth.

The bird is naturally shy and usually avoids man, but instances are recorded where it has made its home in a country garden and even in a city lawn.

PL. LVIII.
HYLOCICHLA FUSCESCENS.
WILSON'S THRUSH.

PLATE LIX.

Fig. 1. CIRCUS HUDSONIUS—Marsh Hawk
Circus cyaneus—Northern Harrier

Illustrated by Howard Jones

The eggs are sometimes laid upon the natural debris of the site, without much if any arranging by the birds. But some birds go even further in their architecture and line this rude foundation with grass, moss, hair, and feathers. At best the nest is but an artless affair and shows but the crudest workmanship.

Fig. 2. BUTEO PENNSYLVANICUS—Broad-winged Hawk
Buteo platypterus—Broad-winged Hawk

Illustrated by Howard Jones

Mr. Audubon frequently observed the Broad-winged Hawk and found its nest and eggs. His account of the female, from which he made the drawing for his great work, is certainly remarkable. He discovered her upon her nest, and his brother-in-law climbed the tree, threw his handkerchief over her, and carried her to the ground. The bird was taken to the house and placed on a stick, where she sat motionless during the time Mr. Audubon was drawing her portrait, and even suffered herself to be stroked and accurately measured with compasses without showing any irritation. The Hawk was finally tossed out of the window, when she at once made off to the woods.

Fig. 3. STRIX NEBULOSA—Barred Owl
Strix varia—Barred Owl

Illustrated by Howard Jones

The Barred Owl is a real desperado, and its depredations are as much feared by the country housewife as those of the Great Horned Owl. Each of these birds, when pressed for food, will boldly enter the poultry yard and carry away chickens, ducks, and even young turkeys. A pair of owls will, in a single night, destroy a large number of chickens, apparently delighting in the sport.

Fig. 4. BUBO VIRGINIANUS—Great Horned Owl
Bubo virginianus—Great Horned Owl

Illustrated by Howard Jones

The owl can become a pretty fair architect, constructing a nest as well as the Red-tailed Hawk, but it is generally too careless or lazy to try its skill in this direction. It prefers to take advantage of the labor of some other bird, and, laying its eggs earlier than these birds, it has the privilege of choosing from all nests of the previous year. When a pair of owls takes possession of an old nest, it is renovated only by the addition of a new lining. The nest is generally situated in a tall tree in dark and retired woods.

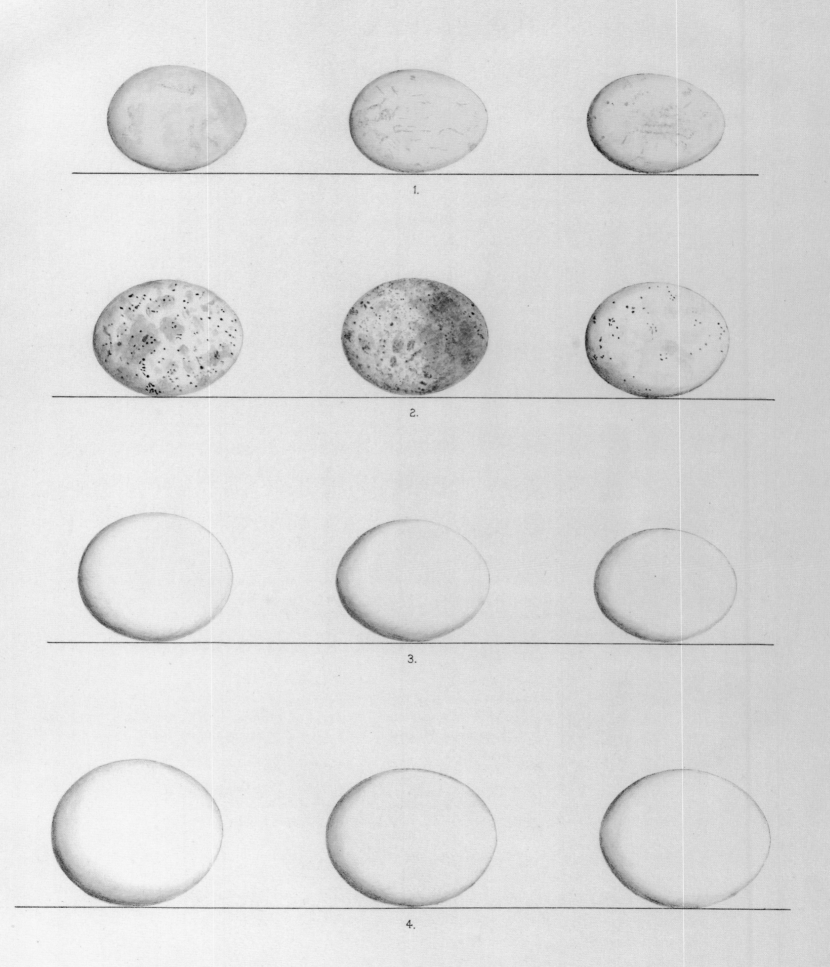

1.

2.

3.

4.

Pl. LIX.

Fig.1 CIRCUS HUDSONIUS.   Fig.2. BUTEO PENNSYLVANICUS.
      MARSH HAWK.   BROAD-WINGED HAWK.

Fig.3. STRIX NEBULOSA.   Fig.4. BUBO VIRGINIANUS.
       BARRED OWL.   GREAT HORNED OWL.

PLATE LX.

Fig. 1. COTILE RIPARIA—Bank Swallow
Riparia riparia—Bank Swallow
Illustrated by Howard Jones

More or less all swallows are colonized during the nesting season, but this character trait is most marked in the Bank Swallow. Those nests which contained the most material also contained the most fleas. The number of these pests in a single nest was astonishing, and it seemed impossible that the mother bird could incubate her eggs under such circumstances. The young, if they had any ideas at all, must have looked forward with something akin to joy to the day when nature would release them from this bondage in "flea land."

Fig. 2. STELGIDOPTERYX SERRIPENNIS—Rough-winged Swallow
Stelgidopteryx serripennis—Northern Rough-winged Swallow
Illustrated by Howard Jones

Although several pairs of the Rough-winged Swallows may build their nests neighboring each other, they do not seem to form a close colony. The mother seems to be willing to take any risk, rather than leave her prospective young. In the fall, after the last brood of young is able to fly, these swallows collect in large flocks. Some days previous to their departure, hundreds may be seen in the air hunting over the water and the adjoining fields.

The two middle eggs show the most common forms.

Fig. 3. PROTONOTARIA CITREA—Prothonotary Warbler
Protonotaria citrea—Prothonotary Warbler
Illustrated by Howard Jones

This Prothonotary Warbler inhabits bottomlands, principally bushy swamps and willows along the borders of stagnant lagoons, or ponds near rivers. Fresh green moss enters largely into the composition of the nest, the shape and size of which varies with that of the cavity in which it is placed. It was made of fragments of dried leaves, broken bits of grasses, stems, mosses and lichens, decayed wood, and other materials. The upper portion consists of an interweaving of fine roots of wooded plants, varying in size, but all strong, wiry, and slender. It was lined with hair.

Pl. LX. Fig.1. COTILE RIPARIA.
BANK SWALLOW.

Fig.2. STELGIDOPTERYX SERRIPENNIS.
ROUGH-WINGED SWALLOW

Fig.3. PROTONOTARIA CITREA.
PROTHONOTARY WARBLER.

Fig.4. COTURNICULUS PASSERINUS.
YELLOW-WINGED SPARROW.

Fig.5. PARUS CAROLINENSIS.
CAROLINA CHICKADEE.

Fig.6. BONASA UMBELLUS.
RUFFED GROUSE.

Fig.7. ARDETTA EXILIS.
LEAST BITTERN.

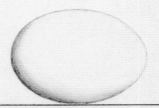
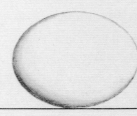

Fig.8. ASIO AMERICANUS.
AMERICAN LONG-EARED OWL.

Fig.9. PHILOHELA MINOR.
AMERICAN WOODCOCK.

PLATE LX.

Fig. 4. COTURNICULUS PASSERINUS—Yellow-winged Sparrow
Ammodramus savannarum—Grasshopper Sparrow
Illustrated by Howard Jones

In *North American Birds*, Mr. T. M. Brewer, writing of the eggs of this species, says: "Wilson and Nuttall describe the eggs as grayish-white, sprinkled with brown. Audubon says they are dingy-white, sprinkled with brown spots." This is not accurate. The ground color is a clear, crystalline white, beautifully dashed and marbled with bold markings of an almost-golden brown. These spots vary in size, are often quite large, and occasionally make a corona about the larger end. Making due allowance for errors of description, there is considerable variation in the eggs of this sparrow.

Fig. 5. PARUS CAROLINENSIS—Carolina Chickadee
Poecile carolinensis—Carolina Chickadee
Illustrated by Howard Jones

Differing from most birds which excavate a hole in decayed or dead timber, the Carolina Chickadee carries an abundance of soft material into the cavity, which is worked into a feltlike lining. When a natural cavity is chosen, the site is often much too large and a great deal more material is demanded than when the builders do their own carpentry, but the internal dimensions of the nest are always about the same.

Fig. 6. BONASA UMBELLUS—Ruffed Grouse
Bonasa umbellus—Ruffed Grouse
Illustrated by Howard Jones

The habitation of the Ruffed Grouse is readily known by a drumming sound made by the male at nearly every season of the year, but most frequently during spring and summer. Little or no art is displayed in building, although great caution and judgment are exercised in selecting the site. How so great a noise can be produced by the exterior of so small an object has called forth much conjecture and contradictory observation. The bird is not destitute of vanity by any means, and it is highly probable from his polygamous nature that the drumming is a special summons or call to distant females to come and witness a display of attitudes, airs, and splendors which are so attractive to the sex, and he may select favorable positions to show off to good advantage.

PLATE LX.

Fig. 7. ARDETTA EXILIS—Least Bittern

Ixobrychus exilis—Least Bittern

Illustrated by Howard Jones

The Least Bittern is the smallest of its tribe, and, to my eye, the most beautiful. Generally it is one of the shyest of birds and is but seldom seen. At the time of mating it is the most animated, and may often be seen climbing about the stems of water plants like the Starling. It flies with like motions to those of the larger members of its family, and as silently as a bat. In the daytime it will seldom fly but a few yards.

Usually the nest is placed near the surface of the water in a cluster of reeds or a tussock of grass, and sometimes also, it is said, in a bush. A dense swampy tract overgrown with cattails and the various coarse swamp grasses is the favorite breeding place of this Bittern.

Fig. 8. ASIO AMERICANUS—American Long-eared Owl

Asio otus—Long-eared Owl

Illustrated by Howard Jones

The Long-eared Owl is exclusively a woods bird, being seldom, I might almost say never, seen in the open. Its habits of life and silence contribute to make it apparently much more scarce than it really is. It is possible to pass close by these birds in the woods and yet not perceive them, as they sit very quietly when one approaches, being either too stupid or too cunning to fly. The whole nature of the bird is retiring and quiet, and in captivity it maintains the same traits, seldom showing a disposition to fight or bite. It is more truly nocturnal than most of the small Owls, hunting entirely by night. With the exception of their love song, which all birds seem to have, it is, I believe, mute.

Fig. 9. PHILOHELA MINOR—American Woodcock

Scolopax minor—American Woodcock

Illustrated by Howard Jones

The American Woodcock is quite universally distributed over the United States. It is noted for its reclusiveness, and no doubt finds in solitude all the charms that sages have seen. If this characteristic is an evidence of wisdom, verily the Woodcock is a solon among the feathered tribes, for it seeks the most solitary and unfinished spots on earth, places where the soil is soft and moist; and here, with no near companion, it passes most of its life in satisfactory if not sweet meditation.

Its nest is a very insignificant affair, yet one which answers the purpose well, as it resembles exactly the surroundings, in fact, is part of them; and since the young run about as soon as hatched, an elaborate structure is not necessary for their comfort. There are no outlines to the structure which are of any value for measurements.

PLATE LXI.

Fig. 1. LANIVIREO FLAVIFRONS—Yellow-throated Vireo

Vireo flavifrons—Yellow-throated Vireo

Illustrated by Virginia Jones

The nest is composed externally of pieces of hornets' nests, vegetable down, lichens, strips of the inner bark of some weed, web from the common plant louse, and spider web, felted together in a promiscuous but firm manner. Within this purse-shaped cavity is a thick layer of bleached blades of bluegrass. The nest is firmly attached to its two supporting twigs by its external layer, which is wrapped around and bound fast to the branches with web.

The eggs illustrated are a little smaller than the average, but they show well the variations in markings. The nest was built in a little wood adjoining an orchard. It is typical in size, shape, and position, but is probably more elaborately covered with lichens than is usual.

Fig. 2. HELMINTHOPHAGA CHRYSOPTERA—Golden-winged Warbler

Vermivora chrysoptera—Golden-winged Warbler

Illustrated by Virginia Jones

The nest was situated under a little bush in a low piece of ground. It rested upon a deep layer of beech leaves, and leaves were piled up around it in a seemingly careless manner, as if blown by the wind. When the leaves are taken away, the nest proper is seen to be made of long strips of grapevine bark, weed fibers, and pieces of beech leaves, and lined with split grasses. The materials are very loosely woven into a purse-like shape, the rear wall being an inch or more higher than the front portion. Woodlands, bushy pastures, and small clumps of timber, provided the soil is damp, are the most frequented nesting places.

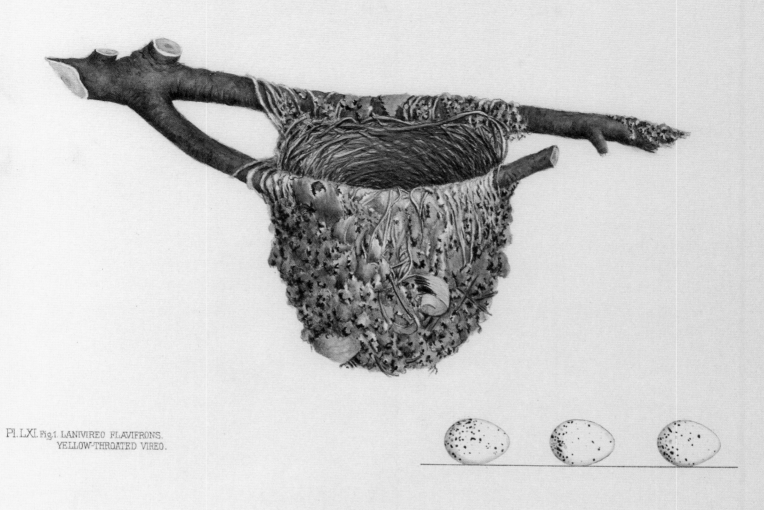

Pl. LXI. Fig.1. LANIVIREO FLAVIFRONS.
YELLOW-THROATED VIREO.

Fig. 2. HELMINTHOPHAGA CHRYSOPTERA.
GOLDEN-WINGED WARBLER.

PLATE LXII.

Fig. 1. QUERQUEDULA DISCORS—Blue-winged Teal

Anas discors—Blue-winged Teal

Illustrated by Howard Jones

These birds are especially fond of muddy pools and ponds overgrown with lilies and rushes. During the spring they frequent the river bottoms, and take great delight in muddy sloughs after freshets. In the fall they feed about ditches and stagnant ponds. When they congregate during midday on the edge of a mud-puddle in perfect quiet, one can walk close to them without noticing their presence, so closely do they sit to the ground and so protective is their coloring.

Fig. 2. BOTAURUS LENTIGINOSUS—American Bittern

Botaurus lentiginosus—American Bittern

Illustrated by Howard Jones

The American Bittern, though shy and retiring, always makes his presence known, and anyone who has lived long in the neighborhood of a swamp inhabited by these birds is familiar with their peculiar and gloomy cry, not at all unlike some ancient bullfrog in sound. Not that the one could be mistaken for the other, but that the same booming, hollow sound characterizes them both.

Fig. 3. AIX SPONSA—Wood Duck

Aix sponsa—Wood Duck

Illustrated by Howard Jones

If the nest of the bird is in a cavity so deep that they cannot climb to the exit, or if unwilling to leave of their own accord, the most curious thing occurs. The mother bird takes her downy brood in her bill, one at a time, and throws them out of the tree. The little fellows, as they obey the law of gravity, extend their legs and wings in an irregular and comical manner; now one turns a summersault, another spins around like a falling autumn leaf, and still another, parachutelike, descends with a sailing motion.

Fig. 4. ANAS BOSCAS—Mallard (a.k.a. Green-head)

Anas platyrhynchos—Mallard

Illustrated by Howard Jones

With the exception of the Wood Duck, the Mallard is the handsomest of all the ducks. Let anyone observe for a short time a full plumaged drake, how proudly he stands among his soberly attired companions, for he is no believer in furbelows and gewgaws of fancy colors as ornaments to the female form. "Awkward as a Duck"? Nonsense! In repose or upon his native element there is not among Nature's store a more graceful bird. He rivals the Peacock in his plumage, and outdoes him in the way he wears it.

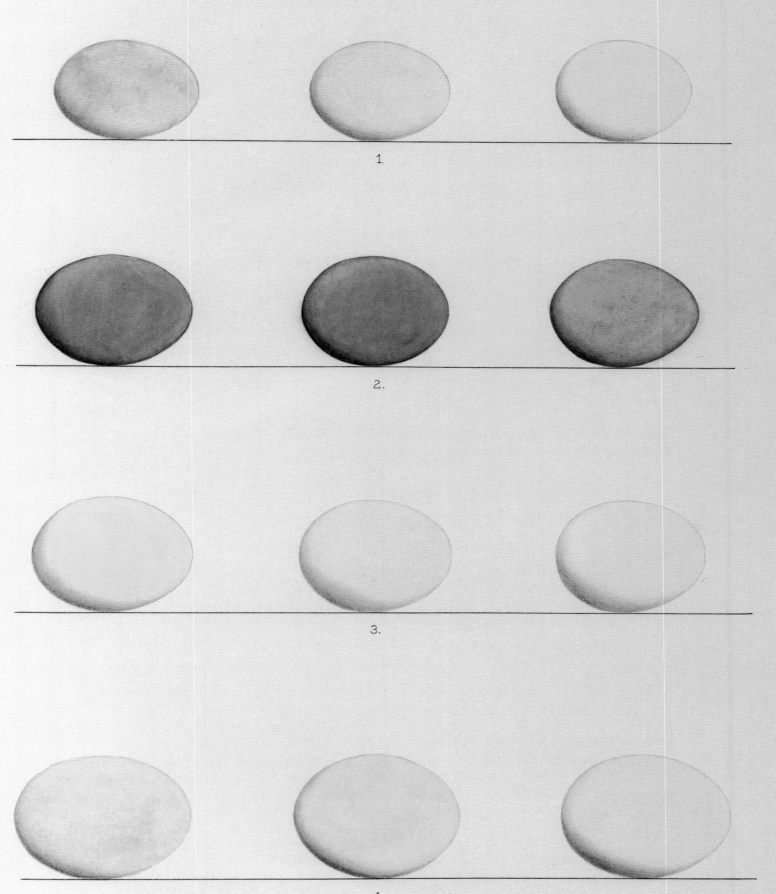

1.

2.

3.

4.

Pl. LXII.

Fig 1. QUERQUEDULA DISCORS.
BLUE-WINGED TEAL.

Fig. 2. BOTAURUS LENTIGINOSUS.
AMERICAN BITTERN.

Fig. 3. AIX SPONSA.
WOOD DUCK.

Fig. 4. ANAS BOSCAS.
MALLARD.

PLATE LXIII.

Fig. 1. ACCIPITER FUSCUS—Sharp-shinned Hawk

Accipiter striatus—Sharp-shinned Hawk

Illustrated by Howard Jones

The Sharp-shinned Hawk attracts the attention of the field ornithologist by the peculiarity of its flight. The rapidity it attains is astonishing, it darts around and through bushes with the speed of an arrow, and like a dart carries destruction in its path.

Fig. 2. PODILYMBUS PODICEPS—Thick-billed Grebe (a.k.a. Dabchick, Water-witch, Dipper, or Diver)

Podilymbus podiceps—Pied-billed Grebe

Illustrated by Howard Jones

The nest is situated either in a bunch of sawgrass or other grass or reeds, or is composed of a floating mass of material anchored in open water.

Fig. 3. CUPIDONIA CUPIDO—Prairie Hen (a.k.a. Pinnated Grouse)

Tympanuchus cupido—Prairie-Chicken

Illustrated by Howard Jones

The eggs under consideration are so characteristic in size, shape, ground color, and markings.

Fig. 4. DYTES AURITUS—Horned Grebe

Podiceps auritus—Horned Grebe

Illustrated by Howard Jones

This odd little bird has the faculty of disappearing beneath the surface of the water when fired at or frightened in any way, and the power of inflating itself with air, thus riding lightly on the water or by contracting its skin and feathers sinking at will to any desired depth. The nest forms a rude mass, always water-soaked and looking like the conventional "last year's bird's nest."

Fig. 5. BARTRAMIA LONGICAUDA—Bartram's Sandpiper (a.k.a. Upland Plover)

Bartramia longicauda—Upland Sandpiper

Illustrated by Howard Jones

It is by no means difficult to find a field containing a pair or two of these birds, but to find their nest is an entirely different matter. As soon as a pair of these birds has reason to suspect that you are about their premises for no good purpose, they begin to mislead you from their nest.

Pl. LXIII Fig.1 ACCIPITER FUSCUS.
SHARP-SHINNED HAWK.

Fig.2. PODILYMBUS PODICEPS.
THICK-BILLED GREBE.

Fig.3. CUPIDONIA CUPIDO.
PRAIRIE HEN.

Fig.4. DYTES AURITUS.
HORNED GREBE.

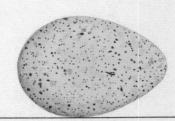  

Fig.5. BARTRAMIA LONGICAUDA.
BARTRAM'S SANDPIPER.

PLATE LXIV.

Fig. 1. PICUS VILLOSUS—Hairy Woodpecker
Picoides villosus—Hairy Woodpecker

Illustrated by Howard Jones

It is one of the most widely distributed species and is subject to innumerable local variations of plumage. Audubon encountered it wherever he went. It seldom associates with other birds, and always appears busy and dignified. The nest of this species is commonly built in an orchard or about the edge of woods.

Fig. 2. CENTURUS CAROLINUS—Red-bellied Woodpecker (a.k.a. Chow Chow)
Melanerpes carolinus—Red-bellied Woodpecker

Illustrated by Howard Jones

This species is probably the most retiring of the family, preferring dense, tall timber to the more open wood frequented by the Red-headed Woodpecker and others, and its nest is generally made in a large dead tree about the outskirts of such timberland.

Fig. 3. PORZANA CAROLINA—Sora Rail (a.k.a. Carolina Rail)
Porzana carolina—Sora

Illustrated by Howard Jones

At best the nest is a poor affair, loosely and poorly constructed, but considering the fact that the young run about as soon as hatched, it is sufficient. It bears a close resemblance to the other aquatic nests. The birds themselves are such consummate adepts at hiding that I would about as soon look for a needle in a haystack as for a Sora Rail in tall grass.

The three eggs show the coloring after the lapse of six years. The nest was on the ground near a spring branch running through wet grassland.

Fig. 4. MIMUS POLYGLOTTUS—Mockingbird
Mimus polyglottos—Northern Mockingbird

Illustrated by Howard Jones

In its favorite breeding grounds of the South, this species has acquired a liking for the habitations of man, and is to be found in greater abundance about dwellings than in dense woods.

Pl. LXIV.

Fig.1.PICUS VILLOSUS.
HAIRY WOODPECKER.

Fig.2.CENTURUS CAROLINUS.
RED-BELLIED WOODPECKER.

Fig.3. PORZANA CAROLINA.
SORA RAIL.

Fig.4. MIMUS POLYGLOTTUS.
MOCKINGBIRD.

Fig.5.ECTOPISTES MIGRATORIA.
PASSENGER PIGEON.

Fig.6. RALLUS VIRGINIANUS.
VIRGINIA RAIL.

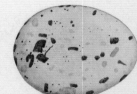

Fig.7. RALLUS ELEGANS.
RED-BREASTED RAIL.

Fig.8.SCOPS ASIO.
LITTLE SCREECH OWL.

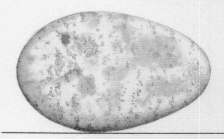

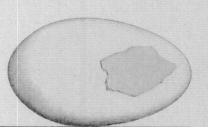

Fig.9.PHALACROCORAX DILOPHUS FLORIDANUS.
FLORIDA CORMORANT.

PLATE LXIV.

Fig. 5. ECTOPISTES MIGRATORIA—Passenger Pigeon (a.k.a. Wild Pigeon)
Ectopistes migratorius—Passenger Pigeon
Illustrated by Howard Jones

I have within my easy recollection seen the sky darkened by Passenger Pigeons during their morning flights to their feeding grounds, and have seen several thousands taken in a single day in a spring-net. Audubon writes as follows in *American Ornithological Biography*: "In the autumn of 1813...I observed the Pigeons flying from north-east to south-west, in greater numbers than I thought I had ever seen them before.... The air was literally filled with Pigeons; the light of noon-day was obscured as by an eclipse; the dung fell in spots, not unlike melting flakes of snow; and the continued buzz of wings had a tendency to lull my senses to repose."

Fig. 6. RALLUS VIRGINIANUS—Virginia Rail
Rallus limicola—Virginia Rail
Illustrated by Howard Jones

The Virginia Rail is a very interesting bird, whether in its wild state or in captivity. When only slightly alarmed, the Virginia Rails utter a chuckling sound, but if badly frightened or greatly annoyed, especially during the nesting season, when they have young, they will emit a sharp squeak, but their regular notes are harsh screams, usually given at night. The young leave the nest as soon as hatched, and run nimbly through the grass. They become scattered somewhat during the day, but toward night they will utter sharp cries, in order that the adults may know of their whereabouts, and then the entire brood will gather beneath the parent for warmth.

Fig. 7. RALLUS ELEGANS—Red-breasted Rail
Rallus elegans—King Rail
Illustrated by Howard Jones

The egg at the left is by far the most common in size, shape, ground color, and marking. The one at the right the next most frequent type, while the middle egg represents an unusually highly colored specimen.

PLATE LXIV.

Fig. 8. SCOPS ASIO—Little Screech Owl (aka Mottled Owl)

Megascops asio—Eastern Screech-Owl

Illustrated by Howard Jones

The Little Screech Owl is essentially a home bird, seldom going far from their abode and remaining in the same place many years. The same hole is often occupied for a series of years by a pair of these owls, in this case there is frequently quite an accumulation of rubbish.

Many writers state this owl can see but little in the day time, an assertion entirely devoid of any facts to support it. Their eyes are unquestionably intended to see with by night, but it does not follow from this that they are blind or nearly so during daylight. The vision of this owl on the brightest day is fully equal to that of a man.

The notes of the Screech Owl are of considerable variety. At certain seasons it annoys the restless sleeper with its weird and tremulous notes. This Owl possesses a love song, consisting of a few simple notes of varying loudness, uttered sometimes slowly, sometimes rapidly, and upon the whole not unpleasing to the ear.

The middle egg is more oval than usual; the others, ordinary in shape, show the variations in size.

Fig. 9. PHALACROCORAX DILOPHUS FLORIDANUS—Florida Cormorant

Phalacrocorax auritus—Double-crested Cormorant

Illustrated by Howard Jones

Cormorants are found in the greatest abundance in the neighborhood of some permanent body of water. They are fierce, pugnacious birds when cornered or wounded, but very shy withal. The nest is usually built in a tree; in places where trees are not available, upon a rocky cliff. The latter would seem to be the more natural locality, but at the reservoirs a dead tree partially submerged seems to be the favorite nesting site.

The eggs are altogether unique in appearance, certainly a partial compensation for their extreme homeliness. Usually there is some small spot upon the shell where the greenish-blue background shows through the outer calcareous deposit, but if this does not exist the lime covering can easily be scraped off with a knife, so as to show the true shell. The egg at the left shows a very rough deposit of lime on the shell; the one to the right shows the color of the true shell, through a break in the outer covering made with a knife.

PLATE LXV.

SIURUS AURICAPILLUS—Golden-crowned Thrush (a.k.a. Ovenbird)

Seiurus aurocapilla—Ovenbird

Illustrated by Virginia Jones

Any visitor to the woods during the months of May and June, must be startled by the shrill *te cha*, *te cha*, *te cha* of the Golden-crowned Thrush, at first uttered so low as to sound at a distance in the bush, and then becoming louder and louder with each utterance, and also more rapid, until it becomes so loud that it is painful to the ear, when suddenly, having reached its climax, it ceases. The author of these notes is difficult to discover, but a little quiet search may perhaps reveal a spotted-breasted little bird perched on some low limb or stepping about upon the ground. He is a homebody, seldom going far from his mate, to whom he repeats his cheering song at intervals. The nest of every Golden-crowned Thrush in the woods may be located within a few yards by observing the singing male, but they are very difficult to actually find on account of their situation and protective covering.

The Golden-crowned Thrush spends most of its time on the ground, searching for food among the decayed leaves. It walks about and scratches in the soft loam like a chicken, instead of hopping like others of its family. It is very attentive to its young, caring for them long after they can fly.

The egg at the left is perhaps the most typical.

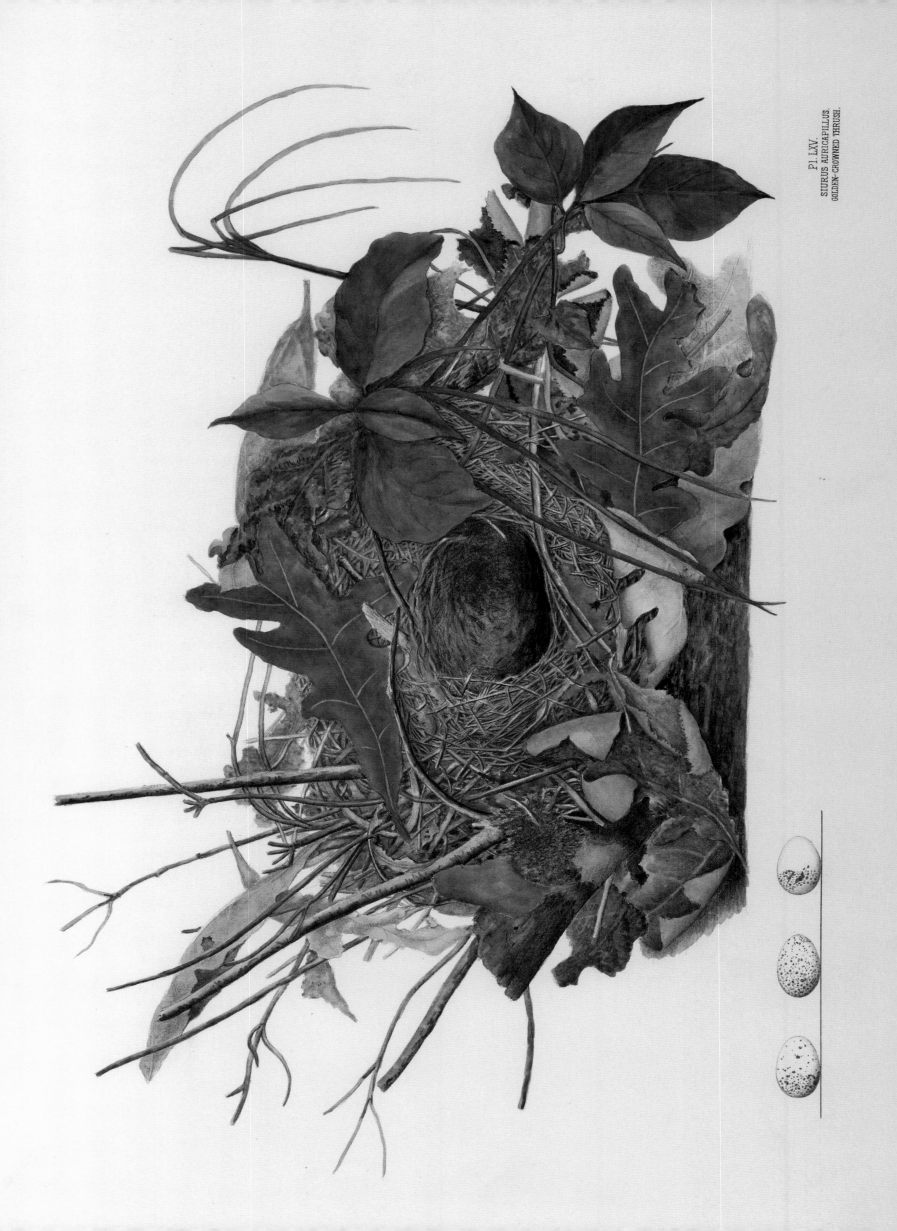

Pl. LXVI.
SIURUS AURICAPILLUS.
GOLDEN-CROWNED THRUSH.

PLATE LXVI.

PARUS ATRICAPILLUS—Black-capped Chickadee (a.k.a. Common Titmouse)

Poecile atricapillus—Black-capped Chickadee

Illustrated by Virginia Jones

Differing from most birds that excavate a home in decayed or dead timber, the Black-capped Chickadee carries an abundance of soft material into the cavity, and forms a soft felt-like nest, in which the mother bird lays her eggs and rears her young. When a natural cavity is chosen, the site is often much too large and a great deal more material is demanded than when the builders do their own carpentry, but the internal dimensions of the nest are always about the same.

The illustrated nest was three feet from the ground in a decayed stump, and the cavity was made by the chickadees. It is composed entirely of moss and very fine downy fibers, the lining being similar to the exterior except that the fibers are more numerous within. Some individuals, either incompetent or hurried, build in a deserted woodpecker's hole or a natural cavity.

Pl. LXVI.
PARUS ATRICAPILLUS.
BLACK-CAPPED CHICKADEE.

PLATE LXVII.

OPORORNIS FORMOSA—Kentucky Warbler

Oporornis formosus—Kentucky Warbler

Illustrated by Virginia Jones

The nest was built in a piece of thickly timbered bottom woods on the ground near an elm sapling, and was unprotected by grass or weeds. Its foundation is composed of dead leaves of elm and oak and of leaf stems. Within this is a superstructure of leaf stems, pieces of slender vine, and rootlets, and this is lined with a compact layer of fine dark rootlets and a few horsehairs.

The egg to the left upon the line is of the most ordinary pattern, while the other two are more unusual in size and markings. It must be remarked that none of these are so extreme as to be uncommon.

Pl. LXVII.
OPORORNIS FORMOSA
KENTUCKY WARBLER

PLATE LXVIII.

Fig. 1. TACHYCINETA BICOLOR—White-bellied Swallow
Tachycineta bicolor—Tree Swallow
Illustrated by Howard Jones

The natural desire of the White-bellied Swallow is for sluggish moving rivers and large ponds of stagnant water. Of the three eggs of the White-bellied Swallow, the middle one is the common size, the others the extremes.

Fig. 2. DENDROECA MACULOSA—Black and Yellow Warbler
Setophaga magnolia—Magnolia Warbler
Illustrated by Howard Jones

It prefers low, heavily timbered woods for its home, selecting for the site a bush or sapling. A nest is a frail affair. Externally is a foundation of light-colored tendrils of a slender trailing vine. Within this basket work is a thicker layer of still more slender, brown-madder-colored vegetable threads of vine, and within this is a lining of hairlike fibers of black moss.

Fig. 3. PARULA AMERICANA—Blue Yellow-backed Warbler
Setophaga americana—Northern Parula
Illustrated by Howard Jones

"Nests [of the Blue Yellow-backed Warbler] in my collection are beautiful structures.... They are composed of long greenish or gray Spanish moss. As a whole, the nest is one of the most curious specimens of bird architecture; the long pieces of moss are woven and twined together in a large, purse-shaped mass." —Oliver Davie, *An Egg Check List of North American Birds*

Fig. 4. SIURUS MOTACILLA—Large-billed Water Thrush
Parkesia motacilla—Louisiana Waterthrush
Illustrated by Howard Jones

Often the nest is placed beside a log, among the roots of a tree, or at the foot of a sapling, usually in the deepest, dampest woods, along streams, about the border of ponds, and in similar places. Of the three eggs, the middle is the pattern most frequently seen.

Pl. LXVIII.

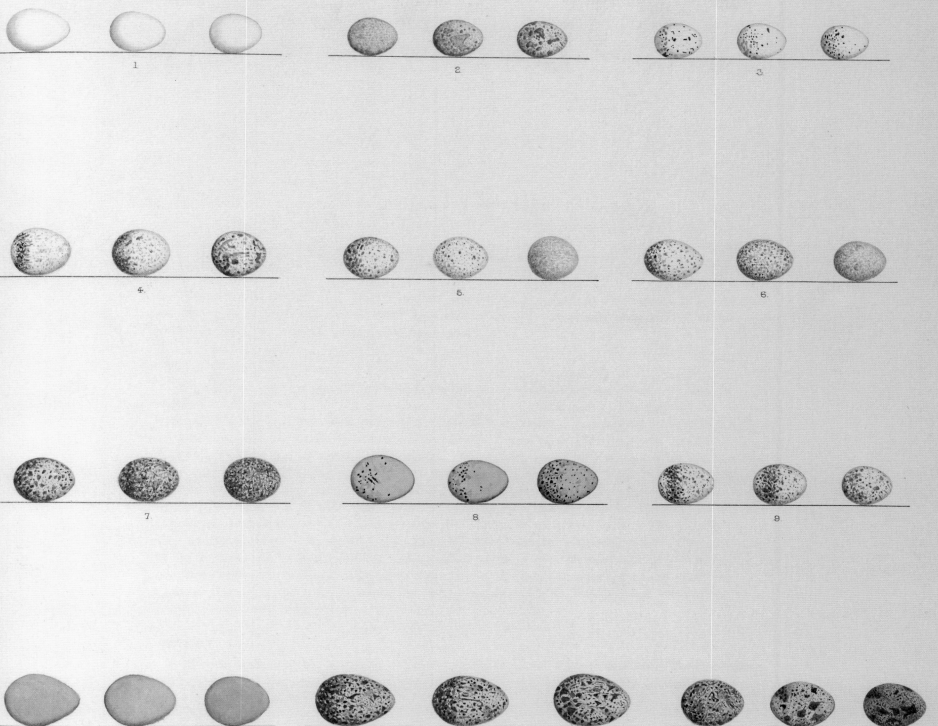

1.

2.

3.

4.

5.

6.

7.

8.

9.

10.

11.

12.

13.

Fig. 13 RHYACOPHILUS SOLITARIUS
SOLITARY SANDPIPER

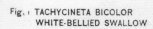

Fig. 1 TACHYCINETA BICOLOR
WHITE-BELLIED SWALLOW

Fig. 2 DENDRŒCA MACULOSA
BLACK-AND-YELLOW WARBLER

Fig. 3 PARULA AMERICANA
BLUE YELLOW-BACKED WARBLER

Fig. 4 SIURUS MOTACILLA
LARGE-BILLED WATER THRUSH

Fig. 5 LOPHOPHANES BICOLOR
TUFTED TITMOUSE

Fig. 6 SITTA CAROLINENSIS
WHITE-BELLIED NUTHATCH

Fig. 7 PASSERCULUS SANDWICHENSIS SAVANNA
SAVANNAH SPARROW

Fig. 8 CARPODACUS PURPUREUS
PURPLE FINCH

Fig. 9 MNIOTILTA VARIA
BLACK-AND-WHITE CREEPER

Fig. 10 HYLOCICHLA UNALASCÆ PALLASI
HERMIT THRUSH

Fig. 11 ZAMELODIA LUDOVICIANA
ROSE-BREASTED GROSBEAK

Fig. 12 DOLICHONYX ORYZIVORUS
BOBOLINK

PLATE LXVIII.

Fig. 5. LOPHOPHANES BICOLOR—Tufted Titmouse
Baeolophus bicolor—Tufted Titmouse
Illustrated by Howard Jones

The nest of this species occurs in nearly every locality, but the favorite place is a tall tree along a riverbank or on a river-island, situations where the soil is continually damp and overgrown with the rankest vegetation. Here this bird selects a natural cavity or the abandoned home of a woodpecker in a part of the tree so high that it rears its young in absolute security from man.

Of the three eggs, the middle egg being perhaps the nearest the average in every respect.

Fig. 6. SITTA CAROLINENSIS—White-bellied Nuthatch
Sitta carolinensis—White-breasted Nuthatch
Illustrated by Howard Jones

From *North American Birds*: "All our ornithological writers have noticed the assiduities of the male bird to his…mate, and the attention with which he supplies her with food. He keeps ever in the vicinity of the nest, calls her from time to time…to receive his endearments and caresses, and at the approach of danger fearlessly intervenes to warn her of it." The egg to the right is the least common in size and markings.

Fig. 7. PASSERCULUS SANDWICHENSIS SAVANNA—Savannah Sparrow
Passerculus sandwichensis—Savannah Sparrow
Illustrated by Howard Jones

"The Savannahs of Florida are wide spread plains.… These salt plains are the resorts of many birds, but none are more abundant there than the little Sparrows which I have under consideration, and which derive their common and specific names from their habit of frequenting savannahs." —Mr. C. J. Maynard, *Birds of Eastern North America*

Fig. 8. CARPODACUS PURPUREUS—Purple Finch
Carpodacus purpureus—Purple Finch
Illustrated by Howard Jones

Within the nest superstructure is a beautifully wrought lining, with walls of the very finest, light-brown rootlets. These are so curly and curved, and interlaced and twisted together at the rim, that the inner nest suggests a piece of silver filigree work.

PLATE LXVIII.

Fig. 9. MNIOTILTA VARIA—Black and White Creeper
Mniotilta varia—Black-and-white Warbler
Illustrated by Howard Jones

When seen in the woods, the Black and White Creeper is generally busily engaged creeping about the trees in search of insects or their eggs and larvae, upon which it feeds almost entirely. It often utters its alarm note if disturbed, or if unmolested, repeats to itself its apology for a song.

Fig. 10. HYLOCICHLA UNALASCAE PALLASI—Hermit Thrush
Catharus guttatus—Hermit Thrush
Illustrated by Howard Jones

Since the young run about as soon as hatched, an elaborate structure is not necessary for their comfort. There are no outlines to the structure which are of any value for measurements.

Fig. 11. ZAMELODIA LUDOVICIANA—Rose-breasted Grosbeak
Pheucticus ludovicianus—Rose-breasted Grosbeak
Illustrated by Howard Jones

"On entering the belt of noble timber that borders the river…we are almost sure to be saluted with the rich, rolling song of the rose-breasted male…the shy and retiring female…is almost sure to be followed the next moment by her ardent spouse, solicitous for her safety." —Dr. Elliott Coues, *Birds of the North-west*

Fig. 12. DOLICHONYX ORYZIVORUS—Bobolink (a.k.a. Reed-bird of the South)
Dolichonyx oryzivorus—Bobolink
Illustrated by Howard Jones

The most remarkable thing about the Bobolink is its song. It has been celebrated in prose and verse until even those persons who have never heard the bird sing must have some familiarity with its notes.

Fig. 13. RHYACOPHILUS SOLITARIUS—Solitary Sandpiper
Tringa solitaria—Solitary Sandpiper
Illustrated by Howard Jones

The Solitary Sandpiper is very retired in its habits, frequenting little muddy ponds in lonely woods and damp, mucky places. The collection of the National Museum (now the Smithsonian Institution) contains five specimens, of which the one illustrated was a part. The others are entirely different in markings.

KEY TO THE EGGS

I. EGGS PLAIN

A. SHELL WHITE OR WHITISH

English and Latin Name of Bird (Contemporary Name)	Size of Eggs, Short Diameter (inches)	Size of Eggs, Long Diameter (inches)	Color of Shell	Number in a Set	Location, Position, Materials, Size, etc., of Nest	Plate Number
American Long-eared Owl *Asio americanus* (Long-eared Owl *Asio otus*)	1.21 to 1.30	1.58 to 1.80	White	3 to 6	Nest consists of sticks, grass, etc., and is placed in a tree, a bush, upon the ground, or on the top of a stump in retired timberland. Often a deserted nest of a crow or hawk is used, and the eggs are sometimes laid in a hollow tree. Eggs in March.	LX
Bank Swallow *Cotile riparia* (Bank Swallow *Riparia riparia*)	.47 to .59	.60 to .72	White	4 to 6	Nest in holes in banks of rivers, etc., usually in colonies and high above the water. Composed of feathers, etc.	LX
Barred Owl *Strix nebulosa* (Barred Owl *Strix varia*)	1.52 to 1.70	1.87 to 2.04	White	2 to 3	Nest in the hollow of a tree or placed in a fork similar to the above. Eggs laid in February or March.	LIX
Belted Kingfisher *Ceryle alcyon* (Belted Kingfisher *Megaceryle alcyon*)	1.00 to 1.06	1.26 to 1.37	Clear white	6 to 7	Nest at the end of burrow in a bank, usually the bank of a river or creek. Commonly bones of minnows and crayfish in the nest. Eggs last of May and June.	XLVII
Carolina Dove *Zenaedura Carolinensis* (Mourning Dove *Zenaida macroura*)	.72 to .92	1.00 to 1.20	White	2	Nest on low limbs of trees and in bushes. Made of sticks, straws, etc.; very shallow. Early in the season, before leaves are out, nest placed on the ground.	XXIV
Chimney Swift *Chaetura pelasgica* (Chimney Swift *Chaetura pelagica*)	.49 to .55	.75 to .85	White	4 to 6	Nest basketlike and made of fine twigs glued together and to the supporting surface by a gummy substance from the bird's mouth. Situated in hollow trees, chimneys, etc.	LIII

Downy Woodpecker *Picus pubescens* (Downy Woodpecker *Picoides pubescens*)	.57 to .67	.78 to .88	White	4 to 6	Nest in holes excavated in dead trees and stumps, usually along the bank of some stream, and from 3 to 10 feet from the ground. Eggs rest on chips and laid in May or June. Diameter of hole at entrance about 1 3/16 inches.	LVI
Great Horned Owl *Bubo virginianus* (Great Horned Owl *Bubo virginianus*)	1.80 to 2.10	2.17 to 2.30	White	2 to 3	Usually the eggs are laid in an old nest of a hawk or in a hollow tree. Occasionally the birds build nests for themselves in the fork of a tree. It is made of coarse sticks, weed stems, etc. Eggs laid in February or March.	LIX
Hairy Woodpecker *Picus villosus* (Hairy Woodpecker *Picoides villosus*)	.68 to .75	.87 to 1.05	White	4 to 6	Nest in holes excavated in dead trees and stumps, usually within 20 feet of the ground. Eggs rest on chips and laid in May or June. Diameter of hole at entrance about 2 inches.	LXIV
Little Screech Owl *Scops asio* (Eastern Screech-Owl *Megascops asio*)	1.18 to 1.25	1.34 to 1.58	White	4 to 6	Nest in hollow trees, at no great distance from the ground. Old orchard trees favorite sights. Eggs from February to April.	LXIV
Passenger Pigeon *Ectopistes migratoria* (Passenger Pigeon *Ectopistes migratorius*)	.98 to 1.08	1.35 to 1.55	White	2	Nest in trees in woods, usually a number of nests nearby each other. Chiefly made of sticks.	LXIV
Pewit Flycatcher *Sayornis fuscus* (Eastern Phoebe *Sayornis phoebe*)	.52 to .62	.70 to .80	White or creamy white	4 to 5	Nest built of mud, moss, etc., about bridges, deserted cabins, caves, etc., and often fastened to the perpendicular side of a rock or timber.	X
Purple Martin *Progne purpurea* (Purple Martin *Progne subis*)	.62 to .74	.90 to 1.02	White	4 to 6	Nest built in natural cavities in trees or, as is now commonly the case, in bird boxes erected for the purpose. Eggs laid in June.	XXVIII
Quail–Bob-White *Ortyx virginianus* (Northern Bobwhite *Colinus virginianus*)	.93 to 1.05	1.13 to 1.30	White, often stained by grass upon which they rest	12 to 30, or more	Nest on the ground in open fields, sometimes in woods, made of grass, etc., and generally concealed from view by rank vegetation. April to July, or later.	XVIII
Red-bellied Woodpecker *Centurus carolinus* (Red-bellied Woodpecker *Melanerpes carolinus*)	.70 to .78	.90 to 1.00	White	4 to 6	Nest in holes excavated in dead trees, high above ground. Eggs rest on chips and laid in May or June. Scarce.	LXIV
Red-headed Woodpecker *Melanerpes erythrocephalus* (Red-headed Woodpecker *Melanerpes erythrocephalus*)	.79 to .89	1.05 to 1.15	White	4 to 6	Nest in cavity in a dead tree, fence-post, stump, etc., excavated by the birds. Rarely in a natural cavity. Diameter of opening to nest about 1 3/4 inches. Eggs rest on chips and laid in May or June.	XLIV

Rough-winged Swallow *Stelgidopteryx serripennis* (Northern Rough-winged Swallow *Stelgidopteryx serripennis*)	.50 to .54	.68 to .76	White	4 to 6	Nest in holes excavated by the birds, in the banks of streams and ponds, seldom more than 3 feet above the water; also in crevices in masonry of bridge piers, etc. Nest of feathers and straw.	LX
Ruby-throated Hummingbird *Trochilus colubris* (Ruby-throated Hummingbird *Archilochus colubris*)	.34 or .35	0.5	White	2	Nest in trees, bushes, and vines, in woods or about gardens and orchards. Nest covered with lichens.	XXV
Ruffed Grouse *Bonasa umbellus* (Ruffed Grouse *Bonasa umbellus*)	1.11 to 1.30	1.40 to 1.70	Milk white to brownish or creamy white, often stained by leaves	7 to 15	Nest of leaves, etc., on the ground beside a log, under a bush, etc., in secluded woods, occasionally in bushy pastures near woods. Eggs from April to September.	LX
Short-eared Owl *Asio accipitrinus* (Short-eared Owl *Asio flammeus*)	1.15 to 1.25	1.22 to 1.58	White	4 to 7	Eggs laid upon the ground or in a little grass, in open, damp, grassy lands. Sometimes they are at the foot of a little bush, beside a log, or in a rabbit burrow. Eggs about April.	XLV
White-bellied Swallow *Tachycineta bicolor* (Tree Swallow *Tachycineta bicolor*)	.51 to .58	.68 to .84	White	4 to 6	Nest of feathers, etc., in deserted woodpeckers' nests and natural cavities in trees near water; also in bird boxes.	LXVIII
Yellow-shafted Flicker *Colaptes auratus* (Northern Flicker *Colaptes auratus*)	.79 to .90	.93 to 1.19	Glossy white	5 to 9	Nest in cavity in a dead tree, fence post, etc., made for this purpose by the birds. Rarely a natural cavity is chosen for the site. Diameter of opening to nest about 3⅛ inches. Eggs in May and June.	LIV

I . EGGS PLAIN

B . SHELL BLUE OR BLUISH, OR GREEN OR GREENISH

English and Latin Name of Bird (Contemporary Name)	Size of Eggs, Short Diameter (inches)	Size of Eggs, Long Diameter (inches)	Color of Shell	Number in a Set	Location, Position, Materials, Size, etc., of Nest	Plate Number
American Bittern *Botaurus lentiginosus* (American Bittern *Botaurus lentiginosus*)	1.40 to 1.60	1.95 to 2.20	Brownish olive green. Dark.	3 to 6	Nest on the ground in weedy and bushy marshes, and in grassy bogs.	LXII
American Goldfinch *Astragalinus tristis* (American Goldfinch *Spinus tristis*)	.50 to .56	.60 to .67	Bluish green tinted	4 to 6	Nest in trees, bushes, and thistles, both in town and country. Usually eggs are laid in July or August, seldom earlier. Diameter of cavity about 2 inches.	XLIII
Black-billed Cuckoo *Coccyzus erythropthalmus* (Black-billed Cuckoo *Coccyzus erythropthalmus*)	.78 to .89	1.05 to 1.17	Pale bluish green	3 to 5	Nest same as the Yellow-billed Cuckoo but a trifle smaller. These eggs and also those of the Yellow-billed Cuckoo may occasionally be found in nests of other birds.	III
Black-throated Bunting *Euspiza americana* (Dickcissel *Spiza americana*)	.55 to .65	.73 to .86	Blue	4 to 5	Nest usually on the ground or near it in a bunch of grass or clover, in open fields. Rarely a nest is built in a bush. Composed of weed stems, grass, etc.	XXIX
Catbird *Mimus Carolinensis* (Gray Catbird *Dumetella carolinensis*)	.60 to .75	.80 to 1.05	Rich bluish green	3 to 5	Nest in bushes and low trees, usually in briers in woods, also in garden bushes, and rarely in orchard trees. Bulky. Composed of sticks and weed stems, and lined with rootlets, etc.	XVII
Cooper's Hawk *Accipiter cooperi* (Cooper's Hawk *Accipiter cooperii*)	1.45 to 1.60	1.80 to 2.10	Greenish blue	3 to 6	Nest in woods, frequently near a pond or stream; high up in trees. Composed of sticks, etc. Eggs around the end of April.	XLIX
Eastern Bluebird *Sialia sialis* (Eastern Bluebird *Sialia sialis*)	.61 to .67	.80 to .87	Bluish tinted	3 to 6	Nest composed of weed fibers, hairs, grasses, etc. Built in natural cavities in woods or open land, also in bird boxes and deserted woodpeckers' nests.	XII

Great Blue Heron *Ardea herodias* (Great Blue Heron *Ardea herodias*)	1.75 to 1.90	2.50 to 2.75	Bluish green	3 to 4	Nest of sticks, etc., in tall trees near water, usually sycamore trees. Often a number of nests near one another. Occasionally nest situated on a rocky bluff.	LIV
Green Heron *Ardea virescens* (Green Heron *Butorides virescens*)	1.08 to 1.20	1.46 to 1.66	Bluish green	2 to 5	Nest in trees or bushes, usually in or near swampy places or streams. Low trees in thickets on islands and in marshes, and also old orchard trees—often at a considerable distance from water—furnish favorite sites. Composed of sticks.	XXVII
Hermit Thrush *Hylocichla unalascae pallasi* (Hermit Thrush *Catharus guttatus*)	.63 to .68	.82 to .93	Greenish blue	3 to 5	Nest on the ground, generally in damp places. Composed of leaves, weed stems, etc.; lined with bark, rootlets, grasses, and sometimes hair.	LXVIII
Indigo Bird *Cyanospiza cyanea* (Indigo Bunting *Passerina cyanea*)	.52 to .59	.69 to .81	Bluish tinted	3 to 5	Nest in bushes and trees in woods, along fencerows, and wherever bushes and weeds grow. Composed of weed stems, fibers, grasses, web, etc. Lined with split grasses.	IV
Least Bittern *Ardetta exilis* (Least Bittern *Ixobrychus exilis*)	.94 to 1.00	1.16 to 1.27	Pale blue	3 to 5	Nest on the ground, in bushes, or, as is usually the case, in a tussock of tall grass in a marsh. Composed of grass, etc.	LX
Mallard *Anas boscas* (Mallard *Anas platyrhynchos*)	1.60 to 1.72	2.12 to 2.30	Greenish or greenish white. Smooth, with an oily texture.	6 to 10	Nest on the ground, in or near wet places. Composed of grass, weeds, feathers, etc.	LXII
Robin *Turdus migratorius* (American Robin *Turdus migratorius*)	.71 to .80	1.00 to 1.20	Blue	3 to 5	Nest in trees, on fence rails, in outbuildings, etc. Always easily recognized by its mud superstructure and lining of blades and grass.	VIII
Wilson's Thrush *Hylocichla fuscescens* (Veery *Catharus fuscescens*)	.58 to .68	.85 to .95	Greenish blue	3 to 5	Nest on the ground or near it in a bush or tussock of grass. Nest and eggs very similar to to the Hermit Thrush. Diameter of cavity about 2½ inches.	LVIII
Wood Thrush *Turdus mustelinus* (Wood Thrush *Hylocichla mustelina*)	.65 to .80	.95 to 1.10	Blue, about the same as the Robin	3 to 5	Nest in bushes and low trees in retired woods. Lined with black rootlets. Superstructure of mud, rotten wood, etc. Diameter of cavity from 2¾ to 3½ inches.	II
Yellow-billed Cuckoo *Coccyzus americanus* (Yellow-billed Cuckoo *Coccyzus americanus*)	.85 to .97	1.13 to 1.33	Pale bluish green	3 to 6	Nest in woods in bushes, trees, and vines. A shallow affair made of sticks, catkins, etc.	XIV

I. EGGS PLAIN

C. SHELL NEITHER WHITE OR WHITISH, BLUE OR BLUISH, NOR GREEN OR GREENISH

English and Latin Name of Bird (Contemporary Name)	Size of Eggs, Short Diameter (inches)	Size of Eggs, Long Diameter (inches)	Color of Shell	Number in a Set	Location, Position, Materials, Size, etc., of Nest	Plate Number
American Bittern *Botaurus lentiginosus* (American Bittern *Botaurus lentiginosus*)	1.40 to 1.60	1.95 to 2.20	Brownish	3 to 6	Nest on the ground in weedy and bushy marshes, and in grassy bogs.	LXII
Blue-winged Teal *Querquedula discors* (Blue-winged Teal *Anas discors*)	1.28 to 1.34	1.76 to 1.90	Creamy or buff	6 to 10	Nest of grass, weeds, feathers, etc., situated in the grass and weeds about the border of a marsh or among the weeds and water grasses of a swamp.	LXII
Horned Grebe *Dytes auritus* (Horned Grebe *Podiceps auritus*)	1.16 to 1.19	1.75 to 1.95	Dirty yellow, with a faint tint of green, often stained by reeds, etc.	3 to 4	Nest of reeds, grasses, etc., either floating on the water of a weedy pond, etc., or placed upon some floating debris. Eggs are covered up by the birds when they leave the nest.	LXIII
Thick-billed Grebe *Podilymbus podiceps* (Pied-billed Grebe *Podilymbus podiceps*)	1.10 to 1.20	1.70 to 1.80	Yellowish brown to olive brown, also milky white, with faint greenish cast	4 to 8	Nest of reeds, grasses, etc., in marshes or placed in a bunch of saw grass. Eggs often covered with mud.	LXIII
Wood Duck *Aix sponsa* (Wood Duck *Aix sponsa*)	1.50 to 1.60	1.70 to 2.10	Creamy brownish or dirty yellowish white	6 to 12	Nest in holes in trees, usually near water. Hollow sycamore limbs overhanging water are favorite sites.	LXII

II. EGGS MARKED

A. GROUND COLOR OF SHELL WHITE OR WHITISH

*With eggs that are marked, it is difficult to tell the actual tint of the ground, owing to the contrast of colors.
The apparent tint is always given. All the very faintly tinted eggs are whitish; but when the tint is quite evident,
the eggs are not included under A, but under to B or C.

English and Latin Name of Bird (Contemporary Name)	Size of Eggs, Short Diameter (inches)	Size of Eggs, Long Diameter (inches)	Ground Color of Shell	Number in a Set	How Marked, Color of marks, etc.	Location, Position, Materials, Size, etc., of Nest	Plate Number
American Redstart *Setophaga ruticilla* (American Redstart *Setophaga ruticilla*)	.45 to .51	.59 to .68	White, often soiled white	4 to 5	Marked chiefly about the base with blotches, spots, and speckles of yellowish brown of various shades. Generally there is a well-marked wreath of confluent markings about the crown. Deep shell marks bluish.	Nest in woods, usually in a sapling against the main trunk, fastened to the bark generally by web. Made of flaxen fibers, web, etc.; lined with horsehairs, and split grasses. Diameter of cavity about 1⅞ inches; depth about 1½ inches.	LI
Baltimore Oriole *Icterus baltimore* (Baltimore Oriole *Icterus galbula*)	.50 to .70	.80 to 1.05	Pure white or faintly tinted with blue or pink	4 to 6	Marked with blotches, dots, speckles, and irregular lines of dark brown or black, usually irregularly distributed over the surface; sometimes the marks form a wreath around the crown. Deep shell marks are indistinct.	Nest pensile, usually near the end of a branch. In woods, towns, anywhere. Made of fibers, strings, etc. Cavity varies in depth from 2¾ to 6 inches; internal diameter at mouth from 2¾ to 3¾ inches.	I
Barn Swallow *Hirundo erythrogaster* (Barn Swallow *Hirundo rustica*)	.50 to .57	.69 to .89	Usually pure white, sometimes dirty or yellowish white	4 to 6	Marked with dots and small spots of slightly reddish brown over entire shell—sometimes thickly, sometimes sparingly, nearly always most abundant about the base. Deep shell marks bluish. Some eggs are blotched with yellowish brown or blackish brown.	Nest usually placed against the rafter of a barn loft, close to the shingles; occasionally on a beam. Built of mud, strengthened with grasses and straws, lined with grass and then with feathers.	XIII
Bewick's Wren *Thryomanes bewicki* (Bewick's Wren *Thryomanes bewickii*)	.48 to .54	.60 to .68	White	4 to 7	Marked with spots and speckles of reddish brown—sparingly toward the point, plentifully about the base, where the marks are often confluent and form a wreath. Deep shell marks are purplish.	Nest in holes and odd nooks about barns, outbuildings, etc.; also in stumps, hollow trees, etc. Made of straw, bark rootlets, leaves, strings, paper, rags, wool, hair, cobweb, and feathers; lined with feathers. Cavity measures in diameter about 2¼ inches.	XLII

Black and White Creeper *Mniotilta varia* (Black-and-white Warbler *Mniotilta varia*)	.50 to .55	.65 to .74	White	4 to 5	Marked with blotches, spots, and speckles of reddish brown, usually most plentiful about the base, where they often form a wreath more or less confluent. Some eggs thickly marked with minute speckles only.	Nest on the ground at the foot of stump or sapling, etc., in retired woods. Composed of weed stems, strips of bark, leaves, leaf stems, etc., compactly pressed and woven together; lined with fine grasses, hair, and sometimes plant down. Some nests are domed. Rarely a nest is built in a cavity in a tree.	LXVIII
Black and Yellow Warbler *Dendroeca maculosa* (Magnolia Warbler *Setophaga magnolia*)	.46 to .62	.50 to .65	Dull white or ashen white	4 to 5	Some eggs are marked pretty heavily with blotches and speckles, others less so, while still others are entirely and uniformly speckled with brown madder or reddish brown. Deep shell marks appear gray. Some eggs look as if color had nearly all been washed off.	Nest in heavily timbered woods, in a bush or sapling, in horizontal or perpendicular fork, from 2 to 10 feet from the ground. Nest is frail, composed of tendrils and slender trailing vines, etc.; lined with slender moss fibers, rootlets, etc.	LXVIII
Black-capped Chickadee *Parus atricapillus* (Black-capped Chickadee *Poecile atricapillus*)	.47 to .52	.58 to .65	White	5 to 8	Marked chiefly about the base with blotches, spots, and speckles of light reddish brown. Some eggs are uniformly marked from point to base. Deep shell marks uncommon.	Nest in natural or artificial cavities in trees, stumps, etc., in woods, etc. Birds usually excavate cavity themselves in rotten or dead wood. Nest within purse-shaped or globular. Composed of moss, hair, and other soft materials, felted together. Cavity about 1⅛ inches in largest part.	LXVI
Blue-gray Gnatcatcher *Polioptila caerulea* (Blue-gray Gnatcatcher *Polioptila caerulea*)	.42 to .49	.55 to .62	White, faintly tinged with greenish blue	3 to 5	Marked with dots, spots, and speckles over entire surface—though most plentifully about the base—with dull reddish brown. Some specimens are marked exclusively with dots of very uniform size; others are marked with large spots. Commonly they are dotted and speckled; occasionally there is a wreath about the crown. Deep shell marks bluish tinted.	Nest in tall trees in woods, etc., saddled on a branch and covered with lichens. External diameter about 2½ inches; depth about the same. Diameter of cavity about 1¼ inches at the rim; an inch below it is nearly ½ inch larger.	XXV
Blue-winged Yellow Warbler *Helminthrophaga pinus* (Blue-winged Warbler *Vermivora cyanoptera*)	.48 to .54	.62 to .70	White	5	Marked with dots and speckles of brown, varying in shade from smoky tint to almost black. Sometimes confined almost entirely to basal half, often distributed regularly over whole shell, never very numerous.	Nest in woods, on the ground at root of weeds, sapling, etc. Composed principally of dead leaves and grapevine bark, lined with fine shreds of bark and split grasses. Diameter of cavity from 2 to 3 inches; depth of cavity the same. Loose and asymmetrical.	XXXII
Blue Yellow-backed Warbler *Parula americana* (Northern Parula *Setophaga americana*)	.48 to .52	.62 to .65	White	4 to 5	Marked with fine spots and speckles of light reddish brown. Deep shell marks lilac. Some eggs are heavily blotched, spotted, and speckled, with a tendency to form a ring around the crown.	Nest in open swampy thickets, among large trees. Nest pensile, 6 to 8 feet from ground; also placed against the trunk of a tree. Composed of long threads of Spanish moss. Entrance often in the side.	LXVIII

Name			Ground Color	Eggs	Markings	Nest	Plate
Bobolink *Dolichonyx oryzivorus* (Bobolink *Dolichonyx oryzivorus*)	.55 to .65	.70 to .90	Dull white	4 to 5	Marked with large blotches, spots, and speckles, and occasionally scrawls of warm, rich brown or a nearly black brown. Deep shell marks gray or purplish and often numerous. Eggs usually profusely marked, sometimes ground color nearly obscured. Shell often looks as if stained.	Nest on the ground in damp meadows, etc. Composed of grass, clover stalks, etc.; lined with grass. Diameter of cavity about 3 inches.	LXVIII
Broad-winged Hawk *Buteo pennsylvanicus* (Broad-winged Hawk *Buteo platypterus*)	1.48 to 1.55	1.90 to 2.00	Soiled white or brownish white	3 to 5	Marked with blotches, spots, and speckles of reddish brown or yellowish brown of various shades. Some eggs are sparingly and regularly marked; others are so heavily marked at one end as to conceal the ground color; others are marked mostly with deep shell marks, which appear lavender.	Nest in trees in damp woods and wooded swamps. Composed of sticks, weed stems, grasses, etc.	LIX
Brown Thrush *Harporhynchus rufus* (Brown Thrasher *Toxostoma rufum*)	.72 to .82	.93 to 1.08	White or white faintly tinted with green	3 to 5	Marked usually with speckles; sometimes with dots or blotches of light cinnamon brown, distributed pretty uniformly and thickly over whole shell; sometimes there is a well-defined ring about the base.	Nest either on the ground or in a bush, hedge, brush pile, or even on a fence rail in the corner of a worm fence—usually in woods but also in open country. Composed of sticks, leaves, weed stems, etc.; lined with rootlets, bulky and coarse. Diameter of cavity from 3 to 3¾ inches.	XXXI
Cardinal Redbird *Cardinalis virginianus* (Northern Cardinal *Cardinalis cardinalis*)	.68 to .78	.90 to 1.10	White; sometimes faintly tinted with green, rust brown, or yellow	2 to 4	Marked with blotches, spots, and speckles. Some eggs are spotted and speckled thickly, almost concealing the ground color, with yellowish brown speckles; others have only a few blotches of rich brown interspersed with faint speckles. Deep shell marks have a lavender tint. Eggs of this species differ greatly even in the same set.	Nest in bushes and low trees, often on a bunch of thorns against the trunk of a honey-locust tree. Composed of long, slender weed stems, grapevine bark, etc., and lined with pieces of slender vine of pinkish gray or brown tint. Diameter of cavity varies from 2¾ to 3¼ inches.	XXII
Carolina Chickadee *Parus carolinensis* (Carolina Chickadee *Poecile carolinensis*)	.45 to .51	.54 to .64	White	5 to 7	Marked with blotches, spots, and speckles, and often short fine lines of light reddish brown. Deep shell marks fainter brown or lavender tint. Some eggs are chiefly spotted at the base; others are blotched at the base and spotted and speckled regularly, but not very plentifully elsewhere: others are pretty heavily marked all over but most abundantly at the base.	Nest in woods or about wooded banks of streams, etc., placed in a natural or artificial cavity in a tree or stump, or in cavity made by the birds themselves in dead or rotten wood. Composed of soft fibers, moss, hair, feathers, down, etc. Nest purse-shaped or globular, felted and woven. Diameter of cavity about 1⅛ inches in widest part.	LX

Bird			Ground color	Number	Markings	Nest	Plate
Chestnut-sided Warbler *Dendroeca pennsylvanica* (Chestnut-sided Warbler *Dendroica pensylvanica*)	.46 to .51	.57 to .69	White, with slightest creamy tint, at times faintly tinted with greenish blue	4 to 5	Marked with blotches, spots, and speckles of various shades of brown; sometimes chiefly confined to a ring about the crown; sometimes distributed pretty evenly over entire shell; at others chiefly on the basal half. Deep shell marks lavender, often numerous, with surface marks superimposed on them.	Nest in saplings and bushes in retired woods, situated in a fork. Composed of strips of inner bark of trees and weeds, and grass, etc., mostly fibers. Lined with wiry threads of grapevine bark, horsehairs, etc. Occasionally a nest is nearly pensile. Diameter of cavity about 1⅞ inches; depth between 1¼ and 2 inches.	LVII
Chewink *Pipilo erythrophthalmus* (Eastern Towhee *Pipilo erythrophthalmus*)	.68 to .80	.88 to .98	White, slightly tinted with bluish green	3 to 5	Marked with blotches, spots, and speckles of brown madder. Usually the shell is well spotted and speckled. Ground color often obsured at base where there is slight confluence of marks. Not much variation in patterns.	Nest in woods, usually with heavy undergrowth of bushes, etc. Placed on the ground, except in very wet seasons (then in bushes). Made of leaves, straw, grass, etc.; lined with slender vine stems, nicely arranged. Diameter of cavity about 3 inches; depth from 1 to 2½ inches.	XXXVII
Cliff Swallow *Petrochelidon lunifrons* (Cliff Swallow *Petrochelidon pyrrhonota*)	.50 to .58	.74 to .87	White	4 to 6	Marked with spots, speckles, and occasionally small blotches of various shades of brown, sometimes quite light, sometimes nearly black, not very numerous. Basal half contains the majority; sometimes they form a wreath, seldom confluent.	Nest placed on the outside of barns and other buildings, under the eaves, or some such place sheltered from rain. Composed entirely of mud, made so as to form a cavity entered only through a small hole. Usually birds build in colonies.	XLI
Cowbird *Molothrus ater* (Brown-headed Cowbird *Molothrus ater*)	.59 to .66	.78 to .90	White, but often obscured by the abundance of the markings	1 to 3 to a nest	Marked with spots and speckles, evenly and plentifully over entire shell together with a few blotches about the base. Speckles predominate on most eggs. Color of marks is very uniform, being brown, inclined to yellow. Deep shell marks have a bluish cast.	Eggs found in any of the smaller nests of other birds, also occasionally in nests of birds the size of a robin.	LIV
Field Sparrow *Spizella pusilla* (Field Sparrow *Spizella pusilla*)	.50 to .55	.61 to .70	White or white with the faintest hint of greenish blue	4 to 5	Marked with blotches, dots, and minute speckles of light reddish brown or yellowish brown over entire egg but most abundant about the base, often forming a wreath. Deep shell marks appear purplish.	Nest in woods, on the ground or in bushes, especially rose bushes. Composed of weed stalks, split grass, roller grass, rootlets, etc.; lined with black horsehair or split grass. Diameter of cavity from 1⅞ to 2½ inches; depth of cavity about ½ inch.	XVI
Fish Hawk *Pandion haliaetus carolinensis* (Osprey *Pandion haliaetus*)	1.75 to 1.90	2.20 to 2.60	Creamy white	2 to 3	Marked with large blotches, spots, and speckles, varying in different specimens from a wine red to purplish brown, usually brown madder. Deep shell marks vary from blue gray to smoky brown. There is great diversity of pattern among these eggs. Occasionally markings obscure ground color entirely.	Nest entirely of sticks, woven into a strong platform and repaired from year to year. Built on the top of a tree.	XXXIX

Golden-crowned Thrush *Siurus auricapillus* (Ovenbird *Seiurus aurocapilla*)	.50 to .60	.76 to .84	White	4 to 5	Marked with blotches, spots, and speckles of different shades of reddish brown. Deep shell marks appear gray. Markings generally limited to larger end; sometimes they are confluent and form a wreath.	Nest in woods with heavy undergrowth, on the ground. Oven-shaped usually, entrance at the side. Composed of leaves, grass, twigs, hair, lichens, moss, etc.; lined with grass. Diameter of cavity from 3 to 3½ inches.	LXV
Golden-winged Warbler *Helminthophaga chrysoptera* (Golden-winged Warbler *Vermivora chrysoptera*)	.49 to .55	.63 to .70	White	4 to 5	Marked sparsely with spots, dots, and speckles of Van Dyke brown, inclined to form a wreath at the base. Some eggs have blotches of washed-out-looking brown.	Nest in woodland, bushy pastures, etc., on the ground at the root of a bush or sapling, or in a tussock of grass or weeds, usually in swampy places. Composed of leaves, strips of grapevine bark, weed fibers, and lined with split grasses. Inside diameter about 2⅛ inches; depth about 3⅛ inches.	LXI
Grass Finch *Pooecetes gramineus* (Vesper Sparrow *Pooecetes gramineus*)	.57 to .68	.76 to .84	White, with faint pinkish or grayish tint	4 to 6	Markings variable. Some eggs are blotched, spotted, and speckled with sepia (almost black), interspersed with coarse, irregular lines. Some eggs have, in addition, faint rusty-brown blotches and spots; some are marked with rusty brown only, thickly sprinkled over the entire shell, so as nearly to obscure the ground color.	Nest usually in a bare field, here and there, with little clumps of grass or weeds. Always on the ground, in a slight cavity. Composed of weed stems, grasses, and straws, etc., entwined and matted together; lined with grasses, rootlets, and horsehairs. Average diameter of cavity 2⅞ inches; depth about ¾ inch.	XLVIII
Great Carolina Wren *Thryothorus ludovicianus* (Carolina Wren *Thryothorus ludovicianus*)	.57 to .60	.69 to .76	White	3 to 9	Marked with blotches, spots, and speckles of reddish brown, distributed over the whole shell, thickest about base, sometimes forming a wreath. Deep shell marks purplish. Some eggs are marked chiefly with large blotches; others are entirely speckled; some have short lines also.	Nest in town or country; often in a brush heap in woods, etc.; generally about old buildings; situated in any unfrequented nook. Made of straw, grasses, weed stems, paper, moss, etc.; lined with grass, feathers, etc. Bits of snakeskin usually to be found in nest.	XI
Kentucky Warbler *Oporornis formosa* (Kentucky Warbler *Oporornis formosus*)	.55 to .58	.72 to .80	White	4 to 6	Marked with blotches, spots, and speckles of reddish brown, with but few deep shell marks; usually marked over whole shell but most plentifully about the base. Some eggs are only speckled. At times all marks are subdued in tone, and the blotches have irregular and indistinct outlines.	Nest in woods with undergrowth of bushes, etc., on the ground at foot of bush or sapling, and in tufts of grass or weeds. Said sometimes to be in a bush. Made of forest leaves rudely thrown together, lined with rootlets, hairs, etc. Diameter of cavity from 2 to 2½ inches.	LXVII
Kingbird *Tyrannus carolinensis* (Eastern Kingbird *Tyrannus tyrannus*)	.63 to .75	.85 to 1.02	Creamy white	4 to 6	Marked with dots and blotches of chocolate brown, irregularly distributed over whole surface or confined to crown—not very numerous. Deep shell marks purplish.	Nest placed in horizontal or perpendicular fork of tree, usually near water. Old apple trees and trees along country roads are favorite sites. Seldom in town. Nest rather bulky, made of grasses, weed stems, fibers, sticks, rootlets, etc., coated inside with rotten plaster, and lined with slender grasses, feathers, wool, etc. Diameter of cavity about 3 inches.	VI

Name	Breadth	Length	Color	Number	Egg markings	Nest	Plate
Large-billed Water Thrush *Siurus motacilla* (Louisiana Waterthrush *Parkesia motacilla*)	.58 to .62	.69 to .79	White	4 to 5	Marked with blotches, spots, and speckles of faint reddish brown. Deep shell marks blue gray. Some eggs have a wreath around the crown, composed of confluent blotches and spots. Often the marks consist of several shades of the same color.	Nest on the ground, among the roots of upturned trees, etc., in dense woods. Composed of leaves, grasses, weed stems, and similar coarse materials, and lined with fibrous roots.	LXVIII
Lark Finch *Chondestes grammica* (Lark Bunting *Calamospiza melanocorys*)	.59 to .67	.76 to .89	White, with sometimes faintest creamy tint	3 to 4	Marked with dots, spots, speckles, and lines of brown, so dark as to be nearly black. Marks beneath the surface appear lavender. The narrower end of shell is usually nearly plain. Lines generally are circular or zigzag and often form a wreath at base.	Nest usually in a poorly cultivated grass field near woods; preferably, recently cleared land. Placed on the ground in slight depression. Composed of clover stems, weed stems, straw, etc.; lined with split grasses or long horsehair. Diameter of cavity 2⅛ inches, depth 1⅛ inches. Nest said to be built sometimes in a bush.	LV
Maryland Yellow-throat *Geothlypis trichas* (Common Yellowthroat *Geothlypis trichas*)	.49 to .55	.61 to .73	White	4 to 5	Marked with blotches, spots, and speckles, and irregular fine lines of sepia. Some eggs are sparingly and others rather abundantly marked. Deep shell marks generally more numerous than surface marks.	Nest in rank grass along the wooded banks of streams, along country roads, in woods and fields, and on the ground among upright stems. Composed of dried leaves, coarse grass, weed fibers, etc.; lined with well-selected blades of grass and roller grass. Diameter of cavity about 2¼ inches.	XXI
Meadow Lark *Sturnella magna* (Eastern Meadowlark *Sturnella magna*)	.76 to .82	1.00 to 1.15	White, at times very faintly tinged with greenish gray	4 to 5	Marked with blotches, spots, and speckles of light yellowish brown or pinkish brown, distributed over entire shell, but most abundant about the base, where sometimes they are confluent. Some eggs marked only with spots and speckles. Deep shell marks are faint and somewhat purplish.	Nest in open fields of grass or small grain, usually in a slight hollow on the ground. Composed chiefly of grass and straw, well woven, and same within as without. Majority of nests are domed. Diameter of cavity about 3½ inches.	XXXVIII
Pewit Flycatcher *Sayornis fuscus* (Eastern Phoebe *Sayornis phoebe*)	.52 to .63	.70 to .80	White or faint creamy white	4 to 5	Marked about the base with a few reddish brown or chocolate spots and speckles. Usually plain.	Nest of mud, moss, etc., about bridges, deserted cabins, caves, etc.; often fastened to the perpendicular side of a rock or timber.	X
Prothonotary Warbler *Protonotaria citrea* (Prothonotary Warbler *Protonotaria citrea*)	.58 to .59	.67 to .73	White	3 to 7	Marked with spots and speckles of dull brown, with faint submarkings of lavender, plentifully and uniformly distributed over whole shell or marked with bold blotches of bright reddish brown, confluent about the base and everywhere interspersed with smaller marks of same color. Eggs blunt.	Nest in natural or artificial cavity in old stump or tree in a bushy swamp, etc. Seldom higher than 15 feet. Made of moss, leaves, twigs, rootlets, etc.; lined with fine rootlets, feathers, etc.	LX

Red-eyed Vireo *Vireo olivaceus* (Red-eyed Vireo *Vireo olivaceus*)	.52 to .66	.75 to .95	White	3 to 5	Marked with spots and speckles, chiefly about the base, with chocolate brown, at times almost black. Occasionally very faint wavy lines in addition. Deep shell marks yellowish brown. From forty to one hundred marks to the egg.	Nest in trees and bushes, seldom higher than 20 feet, usually much lower; generally in woods. Pensile. Composed of inner bark of trees, blades of grass, weed fibers, silken threads, bits of wood, pieces of hornets' nests, etc.; lined with strips of grapevine bark, etc. Diameter of cavity from 2 to 2½ inches.	XXIII
Red-shouldered Hawk *Buteo lineatus* (Red-shouldered Hawk *Buteo lineatus*)	1.60 to 1.80	2.00 to 2.25	Soiled white, occasionally bluish white or brownish white	3 to 4	Some eggs nearly unmarked, others quite numerously blotched, spotted, and speckled with various shades of brown, the ground being obscured at base. Between these extremes are various patterns. Deep shell marks are infrequent. Shell granular.	Nest in tall trees in groves or in woods, frequently near streams or ponds. Composed chiefly of sticks, lined with grasses, moss, feathers, etc.	XLIX
Red-tailed Hawk *Buteo borealis* (Red-tailed Hawk *Buteo jamaicensis*)	1.80 to 2.00	2.15 to 2.60	Soiled white, chalky white, or yellowish white	3	Marked with indistinct blotches and spots of ochre, and variously blotched, spotted, and speckled with reddish or yellowish brown. Deep shell marks purplish; majority of marks are usually on the smaller end. Occasionally an egg is unmarked. Shell is granular.	Nest in trees, generally at edge of thick woods. Sometimes in the interior, often along creeks and rivers. Composed of sticks, lined with corn silks, husks, feathers, grapevine bark, etc.	XLIX
Savannah Sparrow *Passerculus sandwichensis savanna* (Savannah Sparrow *Passerculus sandwichensis*)	.50 to .60	.68 to .80	Dirty white, at times faintly tinted green or blue	4 to 5	Some eggs marked chiefly with speckles of reddish brown; others are blotches, spotted, and speckled; others are mainly spotted; others have ground color nearly obscured by markings.	Nest on the ground in open land, especially in fields of grass and weeds near water. Composed of coarse grasses and lined with finer grass and sometimes horsehair. Internal diameter about 2¼ inches.	LXVIII
Summer Warbler *Dendroeca aestiva* (Yellow Warbler *Dendroica petechia*)	.48 to .57	.55 to .75	Commonly pure white but may be faintly tinted with green or blue	4 to 5	Marked with blotches, spots, and speckles, rarely lines. Yellowish brown or reddish brown of different shades, confined chiefly about the base, where they generally form a ring and are often confluent. Deep shell marks purplish.	Nest saddled on a branch or bush, or placed in a fork. Composed of grayish fibers of plants, felted and woven together; also wool, cotton, etc. Lining usually plant down, with a few horsehairs. Diameter of cavity about 1⅗ inches; depth about 1³⁄₁₀ inches. Very common.	XV
Tufted Titmouse *Lophophanes bicolor* (Tufted Titmouse *Baeolophus bicolor*)	.53 to .57	.66 to .74	White	6 to 8	Marked with spots and speckles, rarely blotches, of brown madder. On some eggs the color is deep and spots large and confluent at the base; others are thickly spotted and sprinkled from point to base—but most plentifully at the base—with light brown madder. Usually they are but sparingly marked, with a tendency to form a wreath at the crown. Deep shell marks not numerous.	Nest in town or country, in hollow trees, crevices in the bark of trees, etc.; also in deserted woodpeckers' nests. Composed of leaves, grasses, lichens, moss, feathers, etc.	LXVIII

Warbling Vireo *Vireo gilvus* (Warbling Vireo *Vireo gilvus*)	.50 to .60	.70 to .78	White	3 to 5	Marked with spots and speckles of chocolate brown, chiefly about the base; about twenty spots and as many speckles to an egg. Some eggs have only two or three small spots and speckles.	Nest in trees, usually near extremity of a branch. Pensile. Composed of long flaxen fibers from the inner bark of trees, weeds, blades of grass, etc.; lined with fine grass, horsehair, etc. Neat and compact. Diameter of cavity at rim about 2 inches.	XXIII
Whip-poor-will *Caprimulgus vociferus* (Eastern Whip-poor-will *Caprimulgus vociferus*)	.80 to .90	1.08 to 1.20	White	3	Marked with large and small spots and some speckles of light yellowish brown distributed rather plentifully and evenly over entire shell. Occasionally a blotch or two occur. Deep shell marks are about as numerous as surface marks and appear lavender.	Nest in densest woods. Eggs laid on leaves on the ground, on a shelving rock, etc. No materials are carried for the nest.	LIV
White-bellied Nuthatch *Sitta carolinensis* (White-breasted Nuthatch *Sitta carolinensis*)	.52 to .61	.68 to .78	White	4 to 9	Marked with blotches, spots, and speckles of brown madder, usually of light tint. Some eggs are sprinkled all over; others have bold blotches in a wreath about the base and are speckled and spotted elsewhere. Deep shell marks grayish.	Nest in trees, generally in the woods; may be in town. Birds excavate a hole high up in trees. Eggs on bare floor of cavity or a nest of hair, feathers, down, fur, grasses, etc., may be built. Nest occasionally in natural cavity.	LXVIII
White-eyed Vireo *Vireo noveboracensis* (White-eyed Vireo *Vireo griseus*)	.50 to .60	.73 to .83	White	5	Marked with a few spots and minute specks of dark chocolate brown or sepia, at times almost black. Marks chiefly about the base. Deep shell marks appear neutral in tint.	Nest placed in a bush or on a low limb of a tree in woods. Pensile. Composed of fibers, bark, leaves, grass, etc. Diameter of cavity about 2⅛ inches in widest part; depth of cavity about 2⅜ inches.	XLVIII
Yellow-breasted Chat *Icteria virens* (Yellow-breasted Chat *Icteria virens*)	.63 to .69	.83 to .96	White	4 to 5	Marked with blotches, spots, and speckles of reddish brown, usually over the entire shell but most plentifully at the base. Some eggs have large blotches of color interspersed with spots and speckles; some have a wreath about the crown.	Nest usually of weed stems, pieces of trailing vines, skeletonized leaves, etc., and lined with well-selected pieces of round trailing vine of a gray, brown, or pinkish cast. Diameter of cavity about 2½ inches.	XX
Yellow-throated Vireo *Lanivireo flavifrons* (Yellow-throated Vireo *Vireo flavifrons*)	.59 to .66	.82 to .95	White	3 to 5	Marked sparingly and mostly about the base with blotches, spots, and speckles of very dark brown. Deep shell marks are gray and sometimes nearly as plentiful as surface marks.	Nest pensile and covered with lichens; placed in trees in woods, orchards, lawns, etc. Rather scarce. Diameter of cavity about 1⅞ inches; depth of cavity about 1⅛ inches.	LXI
Yellow-winged Sparrow *Coturniculus passerinus* (Grasshopper Sparrow *Ammodramus savannarum*)	.56 to .59	.70 to .74	White	4 to 5	Marked with blotches, spots, and speckles of reddish brown. Deep shell marks appear lavender or neutral tint, not very heavily marked. Majority of blotches and spots at the base.	Nest in clover and grass fields, on the ground. Composed of grasses, weed stems, etc., and lined with horsehair and fine bleached grasses. Diameter of cavity about 2½ inches.	LX

II. EGGS MARKED

B. GROUND COLOR OF SHELL BLUE OR BLUISH, OR GREEN OR GREENISH

English and Latin Name of Bird (Contemporary Name)	Size of Eggs, Short Diameter (inches)	Size of Eggs, Long Diameter (inches)	Ground Color of Shell	Number in a Set	How Marked, Color of marks, etc.	Location, Position, Materials, Size, etc., of Nest	Plate Number
Black Tern *Hydrochelidon lariformis surinamensis* (Black Tern *Chlidonias niger*)	.85 to .98	1.25 to 1.35	Olive green, also yellowish or brownish	3	Marked with blotches, spots, and speckles of sepia, so heavy as to appear black. Some eggs chiefly marked with large, distinct blotches and spots; some only with small spots and speckles, confluent about the base. Deep shell marks appear bluish. Eggs often covered entirely with mud.	Nest near large marshes and along rivers, often considerable distance from shore, situated on a muskrat house, an island of reeds, etc. No materials are carried to build the nest—the eggs are laid on decaying vegetation or on the ground.	XLVII
Blue Jay *Cyanurus cristatus* (Blue Jay *Cyanocitta cristata*)	.78 to .84	1.05 to 1.22	Light to dark olive green, sometimes dirty ocherish	4 to 6	Marked with small blotches, spots, and speckles of a darker shade of the ground color, or yellowish brown. Deep shell marks appear purplish. Some eggs are speckled plentifully over the entire shell, the marks being confluent about the base. Usually they are marked with three or four small blotches and five or six times as many spots, interspersed with speckles; majority of marks on basal half.	Nest in trees in country and town, not very far from ground, often in thorn trees. Made of sticks, thorns, weeds, mud, leaves, grass fibers, paper, rags, strings, feathers, etc.; lined with rootlets. Diameter of cavity about 4 inches; depth about 1¾ inches.	XXXVI
Cedar Wax-wing *Ampelis cedrorum* (Cedar Waxwing *Bombycilla cedrorum*)	.57 to .67	.80 to .91	Bluish green or blue gray tinted, speckles sometimes slate color	4 to 5	Marked with well-defined spots, often of sepia, nearly black; marked sparingly but regularly over the whole shell, sometimes forming a wreath about the crown. Usually markings are in small groups. Deep shell marks nearly as numerous as surface marks.	Nest in a medium-sized tree, often orchard or shade tree, in town or country, saddled on a limb or in a perpendicular crotch. Made of rootlets, weed stems, tendrils, fibers, grass, leaves, strings, paper, rags, etc.; lining contains threadlike rootlets. Diameter of cavity varies from 2¼ to 3⅛ inches; depth from 1½ to 2½ inches.	LII

Name					Markings	Nest	Plate
Chipping Sparrow *Spizella socialis* (Chipping Sparrow *Spizella caerulea*)	.49 to .58	.60 to .82	Light bluish green	3 to 5	Marked chiefly about the basal half with blotches, spots, and sometimes lines of various shades of brown, sometimes almost black.	Nest in woods and open country, in gardens, and lawns in town and country, from 1 to 30 feet above ground. Materials vary with locality, usually made of weed fibers, rootlets, grass, etc.; lined with horsehairs. Diameter of cavity about 1¾ inches.	XXVI
Common Crow *Corvus frugivorus* (American Crow *Corvus brachyrhynchos*)	1.10 to 1.25	1.50 to 1.90	Greenish blue	4 to 6	Marked with small blotches, spots, and speckles of bister—on some eggs moderately dark, on others very faint. Marks may be so numerous as to nearly conceal the ground color or may be scattered sparingly. Deep shell marks are purplish.	Nest in trees in woods. Composed of sticks, weed stems, etc.; lined with weed fibers, strips of bark, etc. Cavity well shaped, measuring about 7 inches in diameter and 3 inches in depth.	XLV
Crow Blackbird *Quiscalus purpureus* var. *Aeneus, Ridgway* (Common Grackle *Quiscalus quisicaula*)	.79 to .89	1.08 to 1.20	Greenish blue or smoky blue	4 to 6	Marked with irregular dark brown or black blotches, dots, and lines, and distributed promiscuously over surface.	Nest in trees, among branches, or in a natural cavity. Composed of grass, straw, weed stems, etc., and plastered with mud or manure. Lining, round grasses, and sometimes a little horse hair. Inside diameter of nest about 4⅛ inches.	VII
English Sparrow *Passer domesticus* (House Sparrow *Passer domesticus*)	.60 to .65	.85 to .95	Faintly tinted with grayish blue	4 to 6	Marked with blotches, spots, and speckles, also occasionally short lines of sepia. Some eggs are evenly and thickly marked; some are marked principally at the base; others are evenly but sparingly blotched and dotted.	Nest in any kind of cavity or hole about trees, building, etc. Composed of any accessible material, lined with feathers.	LIV
Field Sparrow *Spizella pusilla* (Field Sparrow *Spizella pusilla*)	.50 to .55	.61 to .73	Faint greenish blue	3 to 5	Marked with blotches, dots, and fine speckles of light reddish brown or yellowish brown over entire egg but most plentifully about the base, often forming a wreath. Deep shell marks purplish. Some eggs speckled only.	Nest on the ground or in a bush in woods. Loosely built of weed stalks, split grasses, roller grass, and rootlets; lined with black horsehairs or split grasses. Diameter of cavity from 1⅞ to 2½ inches; depth of cavity about 1½ inches.	XVI
Florida Cormorant *Phalacrocorax dilophus floridanus* (Double-crested Cormorant *Phalacrocorax auritus*)	1.38 to 1.60	2.25 to 2.50	Greenish blue, but covered almost completely with a thick, white, limelike deposit	3 to 5	Unmarked, except by the limelike wash referred to. Usually the bluish ground color shows at several places.	Nest in trees or on rocky cliffs about lakes, reservoirs, rivers, etc. Usually many nests in same locality.	LXIV
Marsh Hawk *Circus hudsonius* (Northern Harrier *Circus cyaneus*)	1.38 to 1.45	1.76 to 1.86	Faintly tinted with greenish blue	4 to 6	At first glance most eggs seem to be unmarked but close inspection shows numerous blotches of the faintest yellowish brown or lilac. Some eggs are more boldly marked with blotches and spots of light yellowish brown. Eggs often stained by the materials of the nest. Eggs in April or May; shell rough and unpolished.	Nest in open fields near swamps, ponds, etc.; upon the ground, in grass, etc.; sometimes beside a log or under a bush. Sometimes eggs laid upon the debris covering the site; more commonly, grass, leaves, weed stems, and sticks compose a rough nest, which may be lined with moss, hair, or feathers.	LIX

Species					Egg description	Nest description	Plate
Mockingbird *Mimus polyglottus* (Northern Mockingbird *Mimus polyglottos*)	.69 to .79	.87 to 1.00	Pale greenish blue	4 to 5	Marked with bold blotches, spots, and speckles of brown madder or reddish brown. Deep shell marks are lilac. Some eggs are mostly marked with blotches and spots; others are speckled, especially at the base, where, with any pattern, they incline to intertwine.	Nest usually in a low tree or bush in woods or about the outskirts of timber. Composed of reed stems, rootlets, straws, bits of leaves, and pieces of twigs; lined with rootlets, weed fibers, or horsehair. Diameter of cavity about 3½ inches; depth about 1½ inches.	LXIV
Orchard Oriole *Icterus spurius* (Orchard Oriole *Icterus spurius*)	.56 to .62	.72 to .86	Very light bluish green	3 to 5	Marked with a few blotches, spots, speckles, and irregular lines of various shades of brown. Deep shell marks purplish.	Nest in trees, either suspended from extremity of limb or suspended between several upright stems; in orchards or trees in fields, etc. Made of fresh blades of bluegrass, fibers, and strips of bark; generally lined with feathers, wool, plant-down. Cavity measures 2¼ inches in diameter; 2¾ inches in depth.	XL
Purple Finch *Carpodacus purpureus* (Purple Finch *Carpodacus purpureus*)	.53 to .65	.72 to .84	Greenish blue	4 to 6	Marked sparingly, with blotches, spots, and speckles, and occasionally lines of very dark brown, almost black, chiefly about the base. Deep shell marks gray or lilac.	Nest usually in evergreens in lawns in country and town; also in fruit trees, etc. Composed chiefly of rootlets. Diameter of cavity about 2 inches; depth about 1 inch.	LXVIII
Red-winged Blackbird *Agelaeus phoeniceus* (Red-winged Blackbird *Agelaius phoeniceus*)	.63 to .73	.86 to 1.04	Light blue	3 to 6	Marked with spots, speckles, and irregular lines and blotches of dark brown or black, which have a tendency to congregate about the crown. Deep shell marks have a muddy-brown appearance.	Usually nest in tall grass, reeds, or bushes in or near a marsh, but may be in a tree, in woods, or on the ground near damp land. Grasses, reeds, etc., compose the structure. Lining of round grass or split grass, occasionally hairs. Diameter of cavity about 3 inches.	V
Rose-breasted Grosbeak *Zamelodia ludoviciana* (Rose-breasted Grosbeak *Pheucticus ludovicianus*)	.67 to .76	.96 to 1.08	Bluish green, sometimes dull yellowish gray	3 to 5	Marked with spots and speckles of reddish brown, usually in small and diffuse pattern. Some eggs are profusely marked; some have fewer and sharper marks; some have confluent marks at base.	Nest in a tree or tall bush in woods, from 6 to 20 feet from the ground, often in thorn trees. Coarsely built of stubble, leaves, weed fibers, twigs, etc.; lined occasionally with a few horsehairs. Cavity about 3 inches in diameter.	LXVIII
Scarlet Tanager *Pyranga rubra* (Scarlet Tanager *Piranga olivacea*)	.63 to .68	.88 to 1.00	Light bluish green	3 to 5, usually 3	Marked with blotches, spots, and speckles of reddish brown in various shades and combinations. Usually there is a slight wreath about the crown; marks often chiefly on basal half.	Nest in trees in or near woods, from 5 to 15 feet from ground, usually saddled on a limb of several inches in diameter. Composed of weed stems, trailing vines, rootlets, etc. Diameter of cavity from 2½ to 2¾ inches; depth of cavity from ¾ to 1¼ inches.	XXXIII
Sharp-shinned Hawk *Accipiter fuscus* (Sharp-shinned Hawk *Accipiter striatus*)	1.10 to 1.18	1.35 to 1.45	Faint greenish blue, almost white at times	3 to 5	Marked with very large blotches, irregular lines, and spots and speckles of various shades of brown. The largest marks are the lightest in tint. Deep shell marks neutral tint; largest blotches often about the equator.	Nest in fork of tree in dense woods; rarely in a cavity in a tree or on a shelving rock. Composed of sticks, weeds, moss, and sometimes feathers, when in a tree.	LXIII

Song Sparrow *Melospiza melodia* (Song Sparrow *Melospiza melodia*)	.52 to .60	.70 to .83	Faint dull blue, sometimes decidedly blue, occasionally nearly brown	3 to 6	Quantity of markings vary from a few blotches and spots to such a number as to nearly obscure the ground color. Some eggs have a wreath around the crown made of either confluent or separate blotches, etc.; others are uniformly and closely speckled. Between these extremes various combinations are common. Markings are reddish brown.	Nest on the ground, in stunted trees, bushes, drift piles, etc. Made of weed stems, roots, blades of grass, straw, bits of dead leaves, etc.; lined with slender blades of grass, split grasses, and long horsehair. Diameter of cavity from 2¼ to 2¾ inches; depth from 1¼ to 2 inches.	XXX
Summer Redbird *Pyranga aestiva* (Summer Tanager *Piranga aestiva*)	.61 to .70	.85 to .93	Light bluish green, varying in purity and shade in different sets	3 to 5, usually 3	Marked with blotches, spots, and speckles of yellowish brown over whole shell. About the crown there is generally a slight wreath of confluent marks. The blotches and dots have ragged outlines and less color at the edges than in center. Deep shell marks dull purplish.	Nest in woods, from 5 to 25 feet above ground, generally at end of limb, supported by a number of twigs. Made of dead grass, lined with grass. Diameter of cavity from 2⅜ to 2¾ inches; depth from 1 to 1¾ inches.	XXXIV
Swamp Sparrow *Melospiza palustris* (Swamp Sparrow *Melospiza georgiana*)	.53 to .58	.69 to .78	Lightly tinted with bluish green, often clouded with brown	4 to 5	Marked with blotches, spots, speckles, and rarely short lines of reddish brown, sometimes nearly burnt sienna. Deep shell marks bluish. Some eggs are so heavily marked as to obscure ground color at the base; some are thickly marked everywhere; some have a wreath about the crown.	Nest generally in a swampy land, on the ground at the foot of a bush or in a tussock of grass, occasionally in a low bush. Composed of grass, weed stems, rootlets, weed fibers, etc.; lined with grass. Diameter of cavity from 2 to 2¼ inches.	LIII

II. EGGS MARKED

C. GROUND COLOR OF SHELL BLUE OR BLUISH, OR GREEN OR GREENISH

English and Latin Name of Bird (Contemporary Name)	Size of Eggs, Short Diameter (inches)	Size of Eggs, Long Diameter (inches)	Ground Color of Shell	Number in a Set	How Marked, Color of marks, etc.	Location, Position, Materials, Size, etc., of Nest	Plate Number
Acadian Flycatcher *Empidonax acadicus* (Acadian Flycatcher *Empidonax virescens*)	.55 to .59	.70 to .79	Light buff or creamy	3	Marked with blotches, spots, and minute specks of chocolate brown or reddish brown, chiefly on the basal half, often forming a ring. Seldom more than twenty blotches and spots; seldom deep shell marks.	Nest in low trees or in the lower limbs of large trees in woods, usually within reach, in a horizontal crotch near the end of a limb. Made of small, round weed stems, tendrils, catkins, etc. A frail affair, supported at sides only. Eggs often may be visible through the bottom. Diameter of cavity about 2 inches.	XIX
American Coot *Fulica Americana* (American Coot *Fulica americana*)	1.22 to 1.32	1.70 to 1.95	Grayish or pale brownish buff	8 to 10	Marked with dots and speckles of sepia, distributed uniformly and plentifully, rarely confluent. Few marks are larger than a pin's head.	Nest in marshes, etc., situated on the ground among reeds, grass, etc., or a foot or so above the water among reeds. Composed of dead reeds, grasses, etc. Rather bulky, shallow.	XLVII
American Woodcock *Philohela minor* (American Woodcock *Scolopax minor*)	1.10 to 1.20	1.44 to 1.65	Brown, varying from a light shade of Van Dyke to bister, also yellowish brown	4	Marked not very plentifully, with blotches, spots, and speckles of a darker shade of ground color, often confluent at the base, where they are the most numerous. Deep shell marks purplish or neutral tint. Eggs from last of February to May.	Nest on the ground in woods. Eggs laid upon a natural arrangement of leaves, or leaves may be carelessly arranged in a depression at the foot of a bush, tree, etc.	LX
Bartram's Sandpiper *Bartramia longicauda* (Upland Sandpiper *Bartramia longicauda*)	1.25 to 1.38	1.75 to 1.90	Light drab or yellowish brown	3 to 4	Marked with blotches, spots, and speckles of dark Van Dyke brown. Some eggs contain a number of bold blotches; others are entirely speckled. The shell is usually pretty uniformly covered; eggs more than ordinarily pointed (the narrower end is more pointed than usual). Deep shell marks not plentiful, in Payne's gray or neutral tint.	Nest in upland fields of grass, clover, wheat, etc., usually near water, on the ground. Composed of a little grass, weed stems, etc., carelessly put together.	LXIII

Black Tern *Hydrochelidon lariformis surinamensis* (Black Tern *Chlidonias niger*)	.85 to .98	1.25 to 1.35	Light yellowish brown or coffee brown, also olive green	3	Marked with blotches, spots, and speckles of sepia, so heavy as to appear black. Some eggs marked principally with large distinct blotches and spots; some only with small spots and speckles, confluent about the base; others have various combinations of these marks. Deep shell marks show bluish upon light ground colors. Markings often obscured by a coating of mud.	Nest near about large marshes, also along rivers, often considerable distance from shore, situated on a muskrat house, an island of reeds, etc. No materials are carried for the nest. The eggs resting on ground or decaying vegetation.	XLVII
Bobolink *Dolichonyx oryzivorus* (Bobolink *Dolichonyx oryzivorus*)	.55 to .65	.70 to .90	Very light gray, drab, olive, or reddish	4 to 5	Marked with large blotches, spots, and speckles; also occasionally lines of warm, rich brown or brown, nearly black. Deep shell marks purplish gray and often numerous. Eggs usually profusely marked; sometimes greatly obscuring the ground color; shell often looks stained.	Nest on the ground in damp meadows, etc. Composed of grass, clover stalks, etc.; lined with grass. Diameter of cavity about 3 inches.	LXVIII
Broad-winged Hawk *Buteo pennsylvanicus* (Broad-winged Hawk *Buteo platypterus*)	1.48 to 1.55	1.90 to 2.00	Brownish, sometimes dirty white	3 to 5	Marked with clouds, blotches, spots, and speckles of reddish brown or yellowish brown of various shades. Some eggs are sparingly and regularly marked; some are so heavily marked at one end as to conceal the ground color; others are marked chiefly with deep shell marks, which appear lavender.	Nest in trees in damp woods and wooded swamps. Composed of sticks, weed stems, grasses, etc. Built in March or April.	LIX
Florida Gallinule *Gallinula galeata* (Purple Gallinule *Porphyrio martinica*)	1.12 to 1.26	1.55 to 1.84	Pale brownish buff	6 to 10	Marked plentifully with small blotches, speckles, and dashes of rich chocolate brown. Markings larger and more numerous toward the larger end.	Nest in marshes, etc., usually supported by the foot stalks of a clump of flags or grass. Floating nests sometimes occur. Composed of dried reeds, weed stems, etc. About 8 inches in diameter at base; 5 or 6 inches high; diameter at top about 6 or 7 inches.	XLVII
Great Crested Flycatcher *Myiarchus crinitus* (Great Crested Flycatcher *Myiarchus crinitus*)	.60 to .72	.80 to .95	Buff or yellowish-clay color	4 to 6	Marked with lines, blotches, spots, and speckles of burnt umber or walnut color. Deep shell marks are purplish or bluish. Eggs are thickly marked. Usually the lines run lengthwise, often crossing one another.	Nest in cavity, natural or artificial, in a tree, usually in woods but may be in an orchard tree in country or town. Nest composed of weed stems, etc., almost invariably pieces of snakeskin are to be found about the rim.	LIV
House Wren *Troglodytes aedon* (House Wren *Troglodytes aedon*)	.48 to .55	.62 to .72	Pinkish or sometimes nearly white	5 to 9	Marked with blotches, spots, and speckles so thickly as to nearly obscure the ground color of some specimens. Some are thickly and uniformly speckled only; others have a ring about the base, composed of blotches and spots, in addition to the speckles elsewhere. But whatever the arrangement of the marks, they are uniformly brown madder. Deep shell marks may be wanting or numerous.	Nest about old buildings, etc., in all kinds of odd nooks; also in natural cavities in orchard and other trees; often in bird boxes. Composed of sticks, weed stems, strings, horsehair, moss, feathers, etc. Diameter of cavity about 2 inches.	L

Bird							
Killdeer *Oxyechus vociferus* (Killdeer *Charadrius vociferus*)	.98 to 1.07	1.40 to 1.48	Smoky buff	4	Marked with blotches, spots, and speckles of brown, at times almost black. Distributed over entire shell, but marks are largest and most numerous on the basal end. Usually eggs contain several blotches, occasionally marked entirely with speckles.	Nest usually near water, along shore, or in recently plowed fields, sometimes in grass or pasture field; always on the ground. Composed of a few sticks, weed stems, etc., carefully laid in a little depression in the ground. Eggs often on bare ground.	XLV
Loggerhead Shrike *Collurio Ludovicianus* (Loggerhead Shrike *Lanius ludovicianus*)	.70 to .82	.90 to 1.04	Dingy yellowish brown	5 to 6	Marked with irregular spots and blotches of darker shade of ground color. Deep shell marks purplish brown. Markings quite uniformly distributed or chiefly about the crown in a wreath.	Nest in orchard trees, hedges, and small trees in open fields—honey-locust trees favorites. Composed of weed stems, grass, weed fibers, feathers, thorns, etc.; lined with flaxen fibers, feathers, wool, etc. Inside diameter 3⅜ inches.	IX
Long-billed Marsh Wren *Telmatodytes palustris* (Marsh Wren *Cistothorus palustris*)	.48 to .53	.60 to .70	Chocolate, often of a pinkish cast. Some eggs are only lightly tinted; others as dark as a grain of browned coffee.	4 to 6	Some eggs are nearly plain; some are heavily marked over entire shell; some have only very fine and indistinct speckles; others moderately large and bold spots and speckles. The various ground colors and different markings combine to make numerous patterns. Marks usually a darker shade of ground color.	Nest usually between 1 and 3 feet above ground or water; placed in a bush, reeds, cattails, or marsh grass. Globular, about the size of a small coconut. Composed chiefly of long blades of grass, interwoven. Found only about swamps.	XLVI
Night Hawk *Chordeiles popetue* (Common Nighthawk *Chordeiles minor*)	.84 to .94	1.13 to 1.30	Light shade of yellowish brown or stone color	2	Marked plentifully over the entire shell with blotches, spots, speckles, and short lines of slate color or yellowish brown.	No materials are carried for the nest. Eggs laid on bare ground or rocks, also on the flat roofs of city houses, etc.	LIV
Prairie Hen *Cupidonia cupido* (Prairie-Chicken *Tympanuchus cupido*)	1.20 to 1.30	1.65 to 1.75	Light clay color, brownish, or yellowish olive	8 to 12	Some eggs are almost unmarked; others are uniformly speckled more or less plentifully with brown.	Nest in tall grass in open prairie land. Composed of grass, weed stems, etc.	LXIII
Red-breasted Rail *Rallus elegans* (King Rail *Rallus elegans*)	1.18 to 1.25	1.58 to 1.63	Reddish, flesh tint, faint yellowish, or grayish	8 to 10	Marked with blotches, spots, and speckles of umber, inclining to brown madder. Many marks are beneath the surface and appear of different tints, depending on their depth. Marks never very numerous.	Nest in marshy places overgrown with grass, flags, reeds, lilies, etc. Composed of grass, reeds, flags, etc.	LXIV
Solitary Sandpiper *Rhyacophilus solitarius* (Solitary Sandpiper *Tringa solitaria*)	.90 to 1.00	1.30 to 1.40	Clay colored or drab	4	Marked with blotches, spots, and speckles of reddish brown, not very unlike the Killdeer.	Nest on the ground in open fields or near the border of a wooded pond, etc. Said sometimes to lay in the nest of the Wood Thrush, etc.	LXVIII
Sora Rail *Porzana carolina* (Sora *Porzana carolina*)	.80 to .90	1.20 to 1.30	Brown, shading in some eggs toward olive or brownish buff	6 to 10	Marked, not very plentifully, with blotches, spots, and speckles of the same color as the ground but darker. Deep shell marks often wanting. When they occur they are bluish gray.	Nest in marshes and about wet patches of ground, either on the ground or on some rubbish. Made of grass, weed stems, reeds, etc.	LXIV

Name				Color	Number	Markings	Nest	Plate
Sparrow Hawk *Tinnunculus sparverius* (American Kestrel *Falco sparverius*)	1.05 to .123	1.30 to 1.85	Burnt sienna usually, may also be almost white, yellowish, or reddish brown	4 to 7	Marked with blotches, spots, and speckles of reddish brown or yellowish brown. Blotches often so large as to cover one-fifth the shell. Generally the marks are few in number, but they may be numerous, especially about the base, where ground color may be obscured.	Nest in trees, in natural cavities, or in deserted woodpeckers' nests. Usually the trees are old, dead, and semidecayed, and stand alone in fields. Eggs in April or May.	XLIX
Spotted Sandpiper *Tringoides macularius* (Spotted Sandpiper *Actitis macularius*)	.80 to .90	1.15 to 1.30	Buff	4	Marked with blotches, spots, and speckles of brown, varying in shade in different eggs from light brown to almost black. Some eggs are heavily spotted; some have a few large blotches of color at the base; and some have bold spots and speckles, increasing in size and number from point to base. Deep shell marks bluish.	Nest on the ground, always near water, in open places. Composed of small sticks, weed stems, blades of grass, etc., placed in a little hollow. Often eggs are laid on the bare ground.	XLV
Traill's Flycatcher *Empidonax traillii* (Willow Flycatcher *Empidonax traillii*)	.51 to .58	.66 to .74	Light buff or creamy	2 to 4, usually 3	Marked with large blotches, spots, and speckles of various shades of chocolate brown, from a light wash to almost black. Number of marks from two to twenty, chiefly about the basal end.	Nest in bushes and low trees in thickly overgrown bottom land, etc.—willow thickets, so dense as to be almost impenetrable, are favorite places—most generally in a perpendicular fork, within reach from the ground. Composed of flaxen fibers, weed stems, etc.; lined with split grasses, roller grass, etc. Diameter of cavity about 2 inches; depth about 1½ inches.	XXXV
Turkey Buzzard *Cathartes aura* (Turkey Vulture *Cathartes aura*)	1.80 to 2.00	2.56 to 3.03	Creamy or light greenish gray	2	Marked with blotches, spots, and speckles of various shades of chocolate brown distributed over whole egg but most plentifully at the base; not often much confluence. Deep shell marks purplish.	Nest in hollow trees and stumps or on the ground in woods, often in unexpected places in upland woods. No materials are carried for the nest. When on the ground, eggs laid on leaves, etc.	XXXIX
Virginia Rail *Rallus virginianus* (Virginia Rail *Rallus limicola*)	.83 to .93	1.15 to 1.30	Light yellow brown	6 to 10	Marked with reddish-brown blotches, spots, and speckles, chiefly about the larger end. Usually there are deep shell marks, violet gray in appearance.	Nest in marshes and about wet patches of ground, either on the ground or on some rubbish. Made of grass, weed stems, reeds, etc.	LXIV
Wild Turkey *Meleagris gallopavo americana* (Wild Turkey *Meleagris gallopavo*)	1.70 to 1.94	2.30 to 2.80	Light soiled buff	10 to 20	Marked over entire shell with spots and speckles, rarely blotches, of a deep shade of the ground color or yellowish brown, most numerous about the base. Nearly every egg has at least one group of spots larger and darker than the rest.	Nest on the ground in woods with underbrush, under top of fallen tree, beside a log, among bushes, etc. A hollow is scratched in the soft loam and covered with dead leaves; on these the eggs are laid.	XXXIX
Wood Pewee *Contopus virens* (Eastern Wood-Pewee *Contopus virens*)	.50 to .59	.65 to .79	Light buff or creamy	3 to 4	Marked with blotches, spots, and speckles of chocolate brown or reddish brown, confined to the base, where they form a ring; often they are confluent. Deep shell marks about as numerous as surface marks and lavender in color.	Nest in trees about the border of woods, on the banks of streams, etc.; also in town in shade trees. Nest situated on upper surface of a limb or in a horizontal fork, sometimes on a dead limb. Nest covered entirely or partly with lichens. Diameter of cavity from 1⅛ to 2¼ inches.	XIX

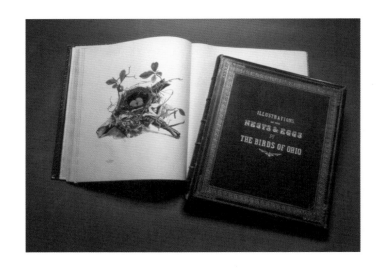

"ASIDE FROM THE ENTERTAINMENT ACCOMPANYING THE STUDY OF BIRDS
in their homes, and the delineation of their various styles of architecture, it has been a great pleasure to us to
continue to completion an undertaking so unfortunately interrupted. It has also been a satisfaction
to us to know that . . . we were breaking ground in a new field, which will yield a rich and beautiful harvest.
If learned ornithologists find in it more to praise than to condemn, we shall be satisfied with our labor."

Howard Jones, Introduction to *Illustrations of the Nests and Eggs of Birds of Ohio*